GETTING OUT OF CONTROL

GETTING OUT OF CONTROL

EMERGENT LEADERSHIP IN A COMPLEX WORLD

NEIL CHILSON

NEW DEGREE PRESS

GETTING OUT OF CONTROL

Emergent Leadership in a Complex World

ISBN   978-1-63676-843-4   *Paperback*

           978-1-63730-199-9   *Kindle Ebook*

           978-1-63730-287-3   *Ebook*

To my daughter Alice. Stay in awe.

Contents

———

INTRODUCTION   11

CHAPTER 1.   THE WORLD IS OUT OF CONTROL   25
CHAPTER 2.   OUR BRAINS, PROSPERITY, AND
             EMERGENT ORDER   41
CHAPTER 3.   WHAT IS EMERGENT ORDER?   63
CHAPTER 4.   HOW EMERGENT ORDER EMERGED   87
CHAPTER 5.   LEADERSHIP WITHOUT CONTROL   115
CHAPTER 6.   YOUR ROLE IN EMERGENT SYSTEMS   135
CHAPTER 7.   EMERGENT LEADERSHIP IN PUBLIC POLICY 153
CHAPTER 8.   CASE STUDIES   185
CHAPTER 9.   YOUR ACTIONS STILL MATTER: THEY
             CAN CHANGE YOU   209
CHAPTER 10. YOUR ACTIONS STILL MATTER: THEY
             CAN CHANGE THE WORLD   225
CHAPTER 11. YOU NEED YOUR COMMUNITIES AND
             YOUR COMMUNITIES NEED YOU   239
CHAPTER 12. SIX PRINCIPLES OF THE EMERGENT
             MINDSET   257

CONCLUSION   263
ACKNOWLEDGEMENTS   271
BIBLIOGRAPHY   273

He was flesh: flesh, bone, muscle, fluid,
orifices, hair, and skin. His body was
controlled by laws he did not understand.

– JAMES BALDWIN, *ANOTHER COUNTRY*

It's an election hall of idiots, for idiots, and
by idiots, and it works marvelously.

– KEVIN KELLY, *OUT OF CONTROL*

Introduction

Are you in control of yourself? Reach your right arm out, point your finger, and touch your nose. If you can do that, you must be in control of yourself, right? But how did that movement happen? How did you move your arm? What signals did you send to which muscles commanding them to contract or relax?

Actually, how did your arm even form? You know it's made from the raw materials you eat at meals, but how did that pizza from last week get turned into your bicep and bone and index finger? You didn't control that process of turning food into your body. No one did. That spectacularly complex chemical and biological feat of turning pizza into muscle (or bone or fat) happened without anyone in charge.

It happened because your body is a ***dynamic, complex adaptive system with emergent properties***. Simply put, your body is more than the sum of its parts. Your body is your own very personal example of the mystery and the power of this book's core theme: emergent order.

But it is only one example. We are surrounded by emergent order—order that occurs without design or control—on all scales. From ant colonies to our brains to our cities to our economies, emergent order is everywhere. Yet we rarely think about this order. Instead, many people casually think about our complex modern world as primarily the result of someone else's design and control.

And increasingly we worry that the world is growing too complex to be under anyone's control. Certainly, the world is getting more connected and complicated. International trade, international communications, and international travel have all skyrocketed. Encountering ideas outside our own experience is as easy as picking up our smartphones. The volume of human knowledge means we rely on experts and specialists more than ever in human history.

Faced with this complexity, we've become obsessed with getting control of ourselves, our jobs, and our families. CEOs want to control their companies; politicians and policymakers want to control the economy. Recently, everyone is trying to figure out what to do to get the COVID-19 pandemic under control.

We want control because as humans, we have a limited ability to comprehend complexity. We're a species that developed in small tribes. For most of human history, the average human never encountered more than a hundred other humans. As a species of tribal animals, we are evolutionarily attuned to be comfortable in small groups. Scientists estimate human brains can only keep track of about 150 relationships and only five of them closely.[1] Historically, our small groups—largely family members—were led by a tribal leader who was like us, shared our perspective and experiences, and therefore could be expected to make decisions with our interests in mind. Therefore, many of us are comfortable leaving hard decisions to leaders. We're built that way. And when chaos arises, we expect the people in charge to restore order.

The instinct to impose order on chaos is human. Humans are goal-setting and tool-using animals. As individuals, we each plan our minutes, hours, days, and our lives. Faced with a deluge of information, we seek to explain, understand, predict, and control the environment around us, in part to improve our planning.

Likewise, in science and politics we often look to experts to design solutions to complex problems. We expect there to be a right answer and for the smartest people to be able to find it. When we see a big problem, we want a big solution. We depend on the people in charge to solve problems that are beyond us, and we're disappointed when they fail.

In our own lives, we also face increased complexity. More choices, more options, more opportunities, more pitfalls. These options are wonderful because they improve our ability to build a life we want. But this doesn't help us decide what that life *should* be. People are searching for a personal GPS to set the destination for their lives and guide them there. We look to rigorous systems of personal productivity, detailed

---

1   R.I.M. Dunbar, "Neocortex size as a constraint on group size in primates," *Journal of Human Evolution*, 22, no. 6 (June 1992).

sets of mantras and codicils, and belief systems in religion or politics. We're attracted to complex systems that promise to make our lives simpler.

Research indicates that people increasingly want tools that simplify and clarify their lives. The self-development industry is predicted to grow 5.6 percent between 2016 and 2020.[2] The market for self-development books and other media, along with self-development apps, personal coaching services, and motivational speakers continues to explode. The rapid growth of personal management and workplace organization applications demonstrates that people want services to manage complexity. Hundreds of productivity apps are available in the Google Play Store and Apple App Store, and articles like "Forty best productivity apps" are common online today.[3] Many of us are looking for that perfect app to help us design a more productive, satisfying life—one that is "in control."

No one is more attracted to the promise of control than the smartest and most successful. When a politician or a regulator encounters public calls for action on a difficult problem, few can say, "This isn't the kind of problem we can fix." Instead, they boldly draft dense legislation and create complex rules. They assemble coalitions to negotiate language that few will read and fewer will understand (there are more than three hundred thousand federal crimes in the US and well over one million regulatory commands at

---

2   John LaRosa, "What's Next for the $9.9 Billion Personal Development Industry," *Market Research*, January 17, 2018.

3   Aaron Brooks, "40+ Best Time Management and Productivity Apps of 2020," *Venture Harbour*, August 12, 2020.

the federal level).[4] But it's not just politicians who fall victim to the illusion of control. Successful businesspeople, leaders, and celebrities often see their success as evidence that they should control things, both in the areas where they have had success, but also in other unrelated fields.

CAN YOU CONTROL THE COMPLEX?

The most ambitious and arrogant of these world builders—tyrants like Joseph Stalin or Adolf Hitler—tried to wipe out history and redesign society from the top down. They failed to wipe out history, but they did murderously wipe out the futures of millions of people. Other schemes to gain control are more modest but still deliver unintended consequences at best. Forced relocation of slums in Mumbai, restrictive zoning in US cities, occupational licensing unrelated to legitimate safety concerns, and risk-averse Food and Drug Administration reviews of vaccines are just some of many examples. Such schemes accrete like rusty sand in the joints of society. The effect can also be deadly, but it is slower and often lacks a baseline for comparison and is therefore harder to recognize.

In our personal lives, the search for control can also be destructive. The continuous tension between the desire to control the world around us and our inability to do so is a great source of stress. Even those who seem to have the resources and power to dictate the world around them cannot control many of the most important things in life:

---

4   GianCarlo Canaparo and Zack Smith, "Count the Crimes on the Law Books. Then Cut Them," *Heritage Foundation*, 2020.

relationships, love, and health. Entertainment news headlines offer many examples of entrepreneurs, organizers, and artists crushing the very thing they most value because they try to control it.

All this destruction begins with misunderstanding how *complex* complex things are. The problem is not just a lack of knowledge. It is that in such complex systems, side effects can swamp intended effects, even for seemingly small changes.

I have been fascinated with the strange characteristics of complex systems since my early teen years. I read two books in those years which shaped the course of my life. The first was James Gleick's *Chaos*.[5] This popular science book explored the then-nascent computer science research into the strange order that underlies seemingly chaotic natural and mathematical systems. From that book I learned about fractals, nonlinear systems, and other messy but still somehow ordered systems. The second book was *Metamagical Themas* by Douglas Hofstadter, which talked about memes, strange attractors, self-referential systems, and complexity theory (among many other things).[6]

I spent hours and hours with these books. I won a science fair in eighth grade with software I wrote to generate strange attractors. These books are why I studied computer science. However, I never could have predicted how profoundly they would influence my personal and professional life.

---

5   James Gleick, *Chaos: Making a New Science* (New York: Penguin Publishing Group, 1988).

6   Douglas Hofstadter, *Metamagical Themas: Questing for the Essence of Mind and Pattern* (New York: Basic Books, 1996).

My teenage self lacked the math skills to absorb all the ideas in these books. But two key ideas from these books permeated into my very core:

Beautifully ordered systems can and regularly do emerge from the independent actions of molecules or cells or people, without anyone being in charge. And in fact, seemingly small interventions into a complex system could send it spinning out of control and even destroy it.[7]

These concepts were fascinating to me but didn't seem to have much practical use when, as a computer scientist and software developer I was writing banking software or studying how to classify the earthquake-readiness of government buildings.

But when I became a lawyer, I repeatedly saw very smart people trying to design rules to govern complex systems with little humility about what success they should expect. Laws and regulations often looked like a series of software patches, each applied to correct the unintended consequences of the previous patch—and each applied with full confidence that *this time* the system was tamed and controlled.

Now, emergent order had something to say. And what it said was that there was a real mismatch between what regulators were trying to control and what they could control.

Meanwhile, I myself became part of the policymaking process. At the Federal Trade Commission, I advised Commissioner

---

7   Neil Chilson, "On 'Beautiful Patterns' and my path toward liberty," *Neil Chilson* (blog), January 21, 2020.

and eventually acting Chairman Maureen Ohlhausen on a wide range of legal cases. I struggled with how to know that I was making things better. What principles ensured that our interventions improved lives, both in the immediate term and over the long term? Again, I leaned heavily on the idea of emergent order when describing whether and what kind of intervention was appropriate as I advised Chairman Ohlhausen.

This idea of emergent order, in my bones from an early age, also shaped my personal practices. As I have transitioned from grad student to lawyer to husband and father, life has grown more complicated. More demands on my time but also less direction on how to spend it forced me to establish habits while accepting the impossibility of keeping everything the same. I became a productivity junkie but still to this day struggle with the insecurity that I am not being as productive as I could or should be. I still wonder how I should spend my time.

FROM POLICY TO THE PERSONAL: THE EMERGENT MINDSET

All of this has shaped what I'll call an "emergent mindset." This is the framework I use to explain, understand, and deal with complexity at home and at work—at both the personal scale and the policy scale. Because I use this mindset as I lead myself and others in both worlds—personal and policy—I'll talk about both in this book.

This is admittedly unusual, but it is wholly intentional. There aren't many books that discuss leadership both in the world of public policy and in private life; typically, these are seen as separate spheres with separate challenges and different tool sets. I intuitively felt that common principles connected these two spheres of life. But it took talking this over with some friends (in particular, my friend Mike Tolhurst) to help me vocalize the connection. Emergent order is ubiquitous in both the personal and public spheres of life. For those who seek to lead, the same principles apply even though the scope of the application differs.

Emergent order links private life and public policy in another way. Policy leaders seek to build systems to protect and empower people. Understanding how emergent order affects everyday life can help policymakers more accurately assess what gaps need filling. It can also help prevent well-intentioned but unnecessary and even harmful policy interventions. This understanding can help policy leaders avoid overreaching into private spheres where their particular tools may not be a good fit.

And from the position of everyday citizens, understanding emergent order can help us step beyond our ingrained, tribal tendency to approach difficult challenges by seeking to control things—or to demand that leaders control things for us. In a rapidly changing world, understanding emergent order can help us improve our personal actions and interactions with our families and communities. It can also alleviate the public's sense of unease that might otherwise drive rash policy choices.

SIX PRINCIPLES OF THE EMERGENT MINDSET

To sum up, there can be order without control. In fact, we see this result constantly, in nature's patterns and throughout human society. This has important implications for leaders in public and private life. Here are six basic principles for leadership in a complex world of emergent order.

- **Expect complicated results even from simple actions.** Complex group behaviors can and often do emerge from many interactions of individual actors following simple rules. Likewise, when we take a simple action expecting a predictable result, if that action feeds into a complex system, we should expect the unexpected. And when we see a complex phenomenon, we should consider whether it is generated by relatively simple individual behaviors repeated many times across many individuals.
- **Don't try to control what you cannot.** Your actions contribute to many larger systems, but usually it's impossible to directly connect your actions to the outcomes. All but the simplest events have multiple inextricably integrated causes. You cannot control what others do, but you can choose how you react. In fact, the only events you have substantial control over are your actions. Focus there, because trying to control what you cannot is a recipe for stress in personal life and a prescription for disaster in public policy. Attempting to exert control isn't just futile; it can actually destroy the very thing you are trying to preserve, like grasping an eddy in a stream.
- **Be humble.** Because you cannot control the results in the world, you should be modest in your promises to others and yourself—particularly if you are making decisions that affect other people's lives. The bigger the potential effect of your decision, the more humble you ought to be when predicting the likely outcome.

- **Push decisions down close to the important information.** Emergent systems work best when there are simple rules at the lowest level possible. Rules can be simpler at the local level because the domain is smaller and there is less need to relay reliable information. Rather than centralizing decision making several levels removed from the facts, empower those closest to the relevant facts to decide.
- **You can make the world better by making yourself better.** You are part of many different dynamic, complex adaptive systems. You have influence, even though you do not have control. But by taking control of what you can—yourself—and letting go of the rest, you can help the various systems in which you participate to become more fitted to their function.
- **Learn from constraints—and choose them well.** Habits and societal institutions constrain us as individuals. Both provide the simple rules that often enable emergent order to produce something complex in our lives and our society. Our habits are the result of feedback loops; when we repeatedly exercise conscious decision-making, we push our complex selves toward a new pattern that can endure in the face of varying conditions. Societal institutions, too, are the result of untold individual choices. We can think of them as the emergent habits, routines, and processes of groups. When we participate in an institution, like a church or a social norm, we help shape and perpetuate it. And the institution also shapes us. We must recognize the wisdom accumulated in such constraints, but without holding them too sacred. We should pick our habits and our institutions carefully and work to develop them.

These principles are not easy to implement. They require a perspective that at once embraces our autonomy as leaders and admits our limitations as part of something bigger. But they offer a chance to productively grapple with the increased complexity of the world and of our lives. If you have ever looked around at the modern world and thought that it is out of control, the message of this book is that you are right! My goal is to help you grow more comfortable with that idea and salvage some personal improvement or fulfillment from it. If you wonder how to think about big policy questions, this book offers a new perspective on the challenges and opportunities of government leadership in an age of complexity. If you are tired of new productivity hacks having temporary effects, this book will help you understand why so many of our attempts to improve fail and how to adapt to that.

Here is how we will approach this journey:

- In Chapters One and Two, we'll explore how life got so complicated, bestowing enormous benefits yet taxing our physical, mental, and organizational capacities.
- In Chapters Three and Four, we'll learn what emergent order is and how the study of emergent order developed.
- In Chapters Five and Six, we'll examine lessons for leadership and where you fit in a world of emergent order.
- In Chapters Seven and Eight, we'll see how emergent leadership applies to public policy and explore two policy case studies.
- In Chapters Nine, Ten, and Eleven, we'll examine why, in a world of emergent order, your actions matter because they can change you, your community, and the world.

- Finally, in Chapter Twelve I'll recap the six principles listed above and show how, based on lessons in the book, you can apply these principles as a leader in public or private life.

Emergent order is a counterintuitive concept to most people. When we seek to lead, we often seek to control. But if we cannot even control the functioning of our own bodies, what hope is there? In an age of increasing complexity, our hope as leaders lies not in gaining control, but in relying on emergent order to help us understand ourselves and our world better and react appropriately. So, how about it? Are you ready to get out of control?

CHAPTER 1

The World Is Out of Control

"We're going a little too fast," I thought, while my then-girlfriend, now wife, Marisa again told me over the phone the address where we were meeting. I was late and in the back of a Washington, DC, cab headed north on Rock Creek Road. That four-lane, limited access road winds alongside a runoff creek, zigzagging through Northwest DC like the scar on Harry Potter's forehead. Despite its twists and turns, Rock Creek Road is often the fastest way to move through Northwest DC and usually is a very pretty drive, with a narrow forest and a steep hill on one side of the road and bikers and joggers winding on the other side on a parallel trail. But it had just rained. The creek was high and turbulent and, as it turns out, the road was quite slick.

"Hold on, we're spinning," I told Marisa, although obviously it was me who needed to hold on. The cab, rounding one of the many turns, had lost traction. It slid off the road, swinging around. The northbound lanes of Rock Creek Road are mostly bordered on the left by a heavy railing and on the right by stone walls or forest. Fortunately, my spinning cab missed all of these obstacles, coming to a rest in one of the very few patches of clear grass, facing the opposite direction we had been traveling.

I don't remember what I told Marisa after the car stopped. I do remember the cabbie apologizing profusely as he pulled back onto the road and drove at a snail's pace for the rest of the short trip.

And I especially remember how my vague anxiety about being in a car under someone else's control crystalized into an icy feeling of helplessness as it became clear that my cabbie wasn't in control of the car, either.

I think many people feel about the modern world how I felt in the back of that cab—the people in charge are letting the world move maybe a little bit too fast. And increasingly many feel like we've already spun out, that no one is in charge and we're going to crash unless we get things back under control.

This feeling is understandable. The world is changing faster than in the past. The Industrial Age spawned technological, societal, and political revolutions. But society has adapted to many of those Industrial Age changes. Throughout the middle of the last century, it often seemed like leaders had a solid grasp on the steering wheel of progress.

But we're not in the Industrial Age anymore. Now we're in the Information Age, and we're facing a new wave of revolutions. Our brains, talented as they are, struggle to keep up.

We face a daily torrent of information and choices that tax our brains' abilities to focus, reflect, and contribute. The wealth of information available to us can seem overwhelming, and it can appear impossible to separate the important and truthful information from the unimportant or false information.

The sophisticated tools we've developed to augment our brains are also under strain. The complex systems that developed in the age of machinery are adapting, sometimes painfully, to the age of computing. Commerce, work, journalism, and government are being reshaped by technology, even as technology adapts to existing social structures.

The exact path is unpredictable. But the trend is obvious: we are exposed to more complexity and we are part of more complex environments where we lack control over the whole.

A WORLD OF ACCELERATING CHANGE

The world is changing faster, becoming more complex, and we sense it. Much of this increase has been driven by information technology, a.k.a. the internet. A good proxy for estimating this accelerating change is the amount of data created. The amount of data created, captured, copied, and consumed was forty-five zettabytes in 2019 and is projected to grow more than five times to 175 zettabytes by 2025. (A zettabyte is one thousand billion billion bytes, approximately the number of grains of sand on the entire earth. It would take 44 billion Blu-ray discs to hold a single zettabyte, a stack that would be 32.8 thousand miles high).[8] This rapid

---

8   "Seagate: Our Story," Seagate.com, accessed February 10, 2020.

acceleration of change, particularly digital change, affects all levels of human experience, from our personal lives to international commerce.

This increase in complexity is global. Supply chains are international, involving thousands if not millions of people from around the globe to produce even seemingly simple products like pencils or T-shirts. Global trade has been one of the great achievements of humankind, moving 1.2 billion people out of extreme poverty since 1990—the fastest reduction of poverty in human history.[9] Extreme poverty has dropped to 10 percent of the world population, down on a constant trend from 60 percent in the 1950s.[10] Extreme poverty is less common in today's poorest countries than it was in the world's richest countries at the start of the Industrial Revolution.[11]

Trade has generated these benefits by making the world increasingly complex. The supply chain that delivers your new Toyota is incomprehensibly convoluted compared to buying a new plow horse from the breeder down the road. Getting your tomatoes from Mexico somehow seems less secure than purchasing them from your neighborhood farmer. Of course, that's just trading one kind of uncertainty for another—a global supply chain protects you from the local hailstorm that, one hundred years ago, could have put a single region into famine.

---

9   Johan Norberg, "Globalization's Great Triumph: The Death of Extreme Poverty," *Human Progress*, October 15, 2018.

10 Matt Ridley, "Ridley: We've Just Had the Best Decade in Human History," *Human Progress*, January 8, 2020.

11 Johan Norberg, "Globalization's Great Triumph: The Death of Extreme Poverty," *Human Progress*, October 15, 2018.

As a result of these changes, the modern world is characterized by an abundance of choice. In the 1960s, a few of the poshest California grocery stores might have had kiwi when in season. Today, the average Midwest grocery store carries kiwis year-round and often has far more exotic produce such as dragon fruit or the giant jackfruit. In fact, grocery stores in the 1960s carried around six thousand unique products; average stores today carry forty-seven thousand unique products.[12]

The massively increased data flows mentioned earlier are likewise an enabler and a result of more choices. Just take a simple question, like what to watch on TV at the end of a workday. In the 1980s, most people had to choose from three or four over-the-air broadcast television networks.[13] Relatively few people had cable, and even if they did, there were only around twenty-eight different cable TV networks. Today, more than nine hundred cable TV networks are available, and there are literally millions of viewing choices on sites such as YouTube, Hulu, Vudu, Netflix, Amazon Prime, and many more.[14] In fact, thirty-thousand hours of new video content are uploaded to YouTube every *hour*—more content than all three TV broadcasters together aired in a year.[15]

The internet has affected far more than just our video choices. It has also fundamentally altered our consumption of all

---

12   "From 1950 to 2010: How the Grocery Industry Has Changed," The Food Industry Association, accessed February 10, 2021.

13   Ron Miller, "The 80s were big for TV," *Washington Post*, December 24, 1989.

14   "Cable's Story," *NCTA*, accessed February 10, 2021.

15   James Hale, "More Than 500 Hours of Content Are Now Being Uploaded To YouTube Every Minute," *tubefilter*, May 7, 2019.

kinds of information. Emails, websites, blogs, tweets, Facebook posts, Wikipedia entries, Medium articles—we have so many more places to gather information from, all of it indexed in search engines and recommended by our friends and algorithms that try to guess what will interest us. Our mobile devices put much of this information within arm's reach, around the clock, wherever we are.

The result is that in our personal lives, we've never had more access to information. And we're still learning how to deal with it. Many of us struggle to get through our work email each day. Social media provides a constant stream of connection—and distraction. Water cooler conversations used to be debates over the latest episode of the same show that everyone was watching. Today, such conversations not only don't happen around water coolers, but they also more often are about what new streaming series to watch or games to play.

Even if the world were not accelerating, the internet has changed how we perceive complexity. Just as global trade has connected our supply chains, the global internet has connected our news sources. The internet means that news about Bombay is readily available, in near-real-time, in Boston or Binghamton. This rush of national and international news means it is easy to perceive a complexity that in the past was hidden by distance and time. This new interconnectedness regularly exposes us to distant events far out of our control.

But the Information Age doubles down on this complexity for another reason: the internet brings so many more buyers and sellers into the marketplace.

One example is online marketing and sales. Sellers face a perpetual challenge: how to identify people who want to buy their product or service. Before the internet, customer discovery was so difficult that only products presumed to have relatively large audiences were produced (one can also look at this from the customer side and say that before the internet it was much harder for customers to find that niche product they wanted). But today, companies can deploy powerful online ad networks to identify and reach audiences for very low cost.[16] This means that producers with very niche products can profitably find consumers. Platforms like Amazon Sellers and Shopify make it possible for very small companies to sell worldwide. Shopify, for example, boasts that "over 1,000,000 businesses in 175 countries around the world have made over $200 billion USD in sales using Shopify."[17] Sometimes these businesses are just one person with a niche idea, like the Polish handmade pinhole camera crafter my father-in-law purchased from. Today's online platforms make it possible for even a lone individual to offer goods and services to international customers. Everyone can run a business with global logistical capabilities.

It has never been easier to get the exact material good that meets your need. Yet all this incredible productivity relies on a complex infrastructure of platforms that facilitate ads, monetary transfers, and logistics, among other things. These platforms provide tools that users can employ to achieve their specific goal, which the platform need not ever know about. On the other hand, the users rarely have full visibility into

16   "The Declining Price of Advertising," *Progressive Policy Institute*, July 8, 2019.

17   "Empowering independent business owners everywhere," *Shopify*, accessed February 22, 2021.

how a platform operates. And many modern transactions span multiple platforms, all interacting with each other. No one person fully understands the process.

All this rapid change and compounded complexity means we have more choices than ever.

MORE CHOICE IS NOT MORE CONTROL

But in this world of countless choices with its many benefits, one thing is crystal clear: an increase in choices is not the same as an increase in control. In fact, increased choice can undermine our feeling of control. Some researchers have referred to this as the paradox of choice, which is the idea that more options can lead to fewer decisions made. The first research articles identifying this counterintuitive result were performed in the early 2000s by Sheena Iyengar. She performed what has become known as "the jam experiments" when she was a doctoral student at Stanford. As a 2010 *New York Times* profile of Iyengar describes the experiment:

> "[R]esearch assistants set out pots of jam on tables in a supermarket—different flavors in groups of six and twenty-four—and offered samples to shoppers. What she discovered was that many of the shoppers who visited the table with the smaller sampling ended up buying jam along with their other groceries, as compared with a mingy few among those who visited the table with the greater selection."[18]

---

18 Penelope Green, "An Expert on Choice Chooses," *New York Times*, March 17, 2010.

Some have used Iyengar's results to argue that consumers should be given fewer choices.[19] But subsequent research has added nuance to Iyengar's results. Scientists have found it difficult to replicate the jam experiment, and a meta-analysis of choice studies revealed that increasing the number of choices has a small or nonexistent effect on average.[20] It also appears that when people know a lot about a category of choices (such as an architect picking building materials), more options are better. And organizing choices into categories can mitigate the paradox.[21]

Most importantly, people develop heuristics and habits to help them deal with a plethora of choices over time. There is a somewhat apocryphal story from the 1980s of immigrants from the Soviet Union who, upon stepping into an American grocery store for the first time, are stunned by the options and paralyzed by indecision.[22] But as Georgetown University philosopher Peter Jaworski pointed out to me, "No one ever talks about the second time those immigrants enter an American grocery store. Apparently, they figure it out!"

Facing a wide array of choices can help people satisfy their preferences more completely than could fewer choices. We

19   Eric Boehm, "Paul Krugman Thinks You'll Be Happier with Fewer Choices. Nonsense." *Reason*, March 2, 2021.
20   Tim Harford, "Given the choice, how much choice would you like?" *Financial Times*, November 13, 2009.
21   "Is the famous 'paradox of choice' a myth?," *PBS*, accessed February 10, 2021.
22   This story may have originated with Boris Yeltsin's very real trip to a Texas grocery store in 1989. Craig Hlavaty, "When Boris Yeltsin went grocery shopping in Clear Lake," *New Haven Register*, September 13, 2017.

also have plenty of tools to navigate downsides, such as reviews. But the takeaway remains: more choice has many benefits, but it is not an unmitigated good.

Joshua Rothman, in a beautiful essay for the *New Yorker*, describes Iyengar's basic conclusion in literary terms. He explores what he calls "the uncanny allure of our unlived lives," the many ways in which we think about what our lives might be like now if we had made different choices in the past.[23] The essay reflects on a book by literary scholar Andrew H. Miller, *On Not Being Someone Else: Tales of Our Unled Lives*. Miller points to "the elevation of choice as an absolute good" and "the increasing number of exciting, stultifying decisions we must make" as increasing the number of lives we do not live.[24] In other words, the more choices we have, the more total curiosity or regret we have about the options we didn't choose.

Modern life is "YOLO + FOMO," as one of Miller's friends put it. We *must* choose because "you only live once" but we *fear* choosing because we have a "fear of missing out" on the opportunities not chosen. The increased number of choices makes us think it may be possible to find the best possible answer, but it also increases the number of paths never taken. No wonder we feel anxious and out of control.

---

23   Joshua Rothman, "What If You Could Do It All Over," *New Yorker*, December 14, 2020.

24   Andrew Miller, *On Not Being Someone Else: Tales of Our Unled Lives*, (Harvard University Press, June 9, 2020).

OUR TOOLS REMAIN INADEQUATE AND EVEN COUNTERPRODUCTIVE

As I've already noted, individuals have tools and techniques that help them manage an otherwise overwhelming amount of choice. Likewise, human society has evolved tools to process large amounts of information. Trusted institutions like government agencies and news media generate, filter, and transmit information, simplifying our own information gathering and streamlining how we make decisions. But the rapidly expanding information ecosystem has strained these institutions.

GATEKEEPERS DISRUPTED

Consider the newspaper industry. Newspapers have long been a core institution in American political, cultural, and social life. Journalism is one of the key filters that helps everyday people identify credible facts and understand developments around the world. Yet newspapers have cut about half of their journalists since 2008.[25]

News-producing companies face a dual challenge from the internet. First, they face competition from an entirely new model of advertising. Ad dollars have long been the fiscal backbone of newspapers. Even though circulation had been declining since the 1950s, newspaper ad revenue continued to climb as page count and number of ads swelled. And because most metro areas have had only one major newspaper since the 1960s, these local monopolies were able to capture a high percentage of the advertising dollars. But in

---

25 Elizabeth Grieco, "U.S. newspapers have shed half of their newsroom employees since 2008," *Pew Research Center*, April 20, 2020.

1996 a new competitor appeared. Online classifieds company Craigslist offered a free online version of classified advertisements, which even today costs five dollars per line in a newspaper.[26] Consumers loved Craigslist. And then in the early 2000s came the rise of personalized online advertising. That created entirely new markets for advertising. Personalized online ads can reach a national or international audience of people who are interested in a product. They simply work better and are cheaper than newspaper ads.[27] As a result, newspaper ad revenue is down 80 percent from its peak in 2000.[28]

Second, the very purpose of journalism has come under question. Journalists used to see themselves as an essential conduit for critical information. "We put out the daily miracle. We saw ourselves as the holders of truth," I was told by Jeff Jarvis, director of the Tow-Knight Center for Entrepreneurial Journalism at CUNY's Craig Newmark Graduate School of Journalism. But things have changed. People no longer rely exclusively or even primarily on traditional media to find news. According to Pew Research, "43 percent of adults get news often from news websites or social media," compared to 49 percent for TV and a mere 16 percent for print newspapers, as of 2018. When separated into age groups, online sources of news dominate younger demographics. Even in 2018, 63 percent of those eighteen to twenty-nine got news often from online sources, with

26 Kathy J. Kobliski, "Classified Ads," *Entrepreneur*, January 17, 2006.
27 Jeff Bercovici, "Sorry, Craig: Study Finds Craigslist Took $5 Billion from Newspapers," *Forbes*, August 14, 2013.
28 Benedict Evans, "News by the ton: 75 years of US advertising," *Benedict Evans*, accessed February 10, 2021.

social media being the largest category at 36 percent. And the downward trends for TV and newspaper news suggest that online is even bigger now.[29]

"Media are no longer the deliverers of information," Jarvis told me. "The information has already been delivered. So the question now for journalists is how—and whether—we add value to that stream of information." To do that, Jarvis has called for a transformation from a mass media business model that spews out volume trying to attract as many eyeballs as possible to a community-focused approach where journalists seek to understand what a specific community needs and deploy journalistic tools to provide that community with the information it needs through conversation, not through a one-way medium.

But the industry has been very slow to transform, even in the face of these threats. Jarvis explained to me that many journalists don't want to relinquish the one-way model where they discover the truth and then share it with the world. And on the business side, newspapers are still invested in the mass media business model that treats all readers as if they have the same information needs. For example, according to Jarvis, newspapers remain loathe to consider personalizing content to readers. Jarvis told me that when he suggests personalization—a way of listening to consumers and delivering what is important to them—newspaper editors would actually get angry at him. "'Subscribers are buying *my* judgment,' they'd say."

---

29 Elisa Shearer, "Social media outpaces print newspapers in the U.S. as a news source," *Pew Research Center*, December 10, 2018.

In short, Facebook, Twitter, Google, and other social media platforms have weakened the ability of a concentrated few to control ideas.[30] This gatekeeper disruption has made it easier for those who want to share new ideas and more complicated for those who want to identify (or dictate) the truth.

This disruption has also triggered complex pressure for these platforms to replace the gatekeeper function that news organizations previously served. Take, for example, the current controversy over how platforms like Facebook and Twitter moderate posts by users. At issue is how platforms should deal with user-posted content that is illegal, offensive, false, dangerous, or otherwise problematic.[31] This could include content like anti-vaccination discussions or attempts at election manipulation. Some platforms are close to free-for-all zones. Others police their content heavily. For the biggest platforms, because they host so much user speech, this debate has taken on a decidedly partisan political tone.[32] It's only a slight oversimplification of the controversy to describe it as "conservatives think social media platforms take down too much conservative content, and progressives think the platforms don't take down enough conservative content."[33] More on the policy implications of this issue in Chapter Eight.

---

30 Neil Chilson and Casey Mattox, "[The] Breakup Speech: Can Antitrust Fix the Relationship Between Platforms and Free Speech Values?, *Knight Institute*, March 5, 2020.

31 Jyoti Panday, "Exploring the problems of content moderation on social media," *Internet Governance Project*, December 23, 2020.

32 Emily Vogels, "Partisans in the U.S. increasingly divided on whether offensive content online is taken seriously enough, *Pew Research Center*, October 8, 2020.

33 Neil Chilson and Casey Mattox, "[The] Breakup Speech: Can Antitrust Fix the Relationship Between Platforms and Free Speech Values," *Knight First Amendment Institute*, March 5, 2020.

Increasingly, we don't trust the traditional gatekeepers or the new conduits for information. Afloat in an ocean of information, we're grasping for trusted sources, and this contributes to our feeling of being out of control.

FACING INFORMATION OVERLOAD

The modern world, with its information pipelines that let us easily discover the wide scale of the world we live in, frequently reminds us that we are each a very small piece of a very large world. From there, it's not a very far step to believe our lives are not under our control.

Our personal encounters with the information world don't offer much solace. These new input streams are novel, interesting, and attractive—even if we aren't quite sure they are useful. People seek tools to control the flow of information. People try to multitask. It seems the only way to possibly keep up. But we're very bad at it—for conscious thinking, our brains do not really multitask; they simply switch between tasks quickly. And each context switch disrupts our work.[34] I know when I'm waiting for a big PDF to load on my desktop, I sometimes hop over to Twitter... and often never hop back.

We deal with this overload in different ways, some of them quite drastic. Indeed, it has become fashionable to cut ourselves off entirely from these information streams. Many productivity gurus call for cell phone siestas or other set times to avoid electronic devices.[35] The term "unplug" has become

---

34 Cynthia Kubu and Andre Machado, "The Science Is Clear: Why Multitasking Doesn't Work," *Cleveland Clinic*, June 1, 2017.

35 Tiffany Shlain, *24/6: The Power of Unplugging One Day a Week*, (Simon & Schuster, September 24, 2019).

synonymous with disconnecting from the internet and is seen as a way to relax and recharge. But unplugging can just delay the overload; just ask anyone who has ever returned from a vacation to an overflowing email inbox.

Indeed, most of us must stay connected for a significant part of our day. How do we handle the firehose of information? Consumers are starting to seek technical tools—and companies are providing them. Both Android and Apple offer controls that limit the amount of app usage, limit notifications, and otherwise let users customize the level of disruption by social media and other apps.[36] Apps like WriteRoom isolate just a writing surface on your computer desktop, eliminating the purported benefits of the windows system in order to boost productivity.

But for many of us, our habits and these tools aren't up to the task yet. We feel overwhelmed with options, unable to choose, and fundamentally out of control of ourselves and the world around us.

The world has sped up. Technology and trade have given us many choices. The complexity of it all can feel very overwhelming. Like my Rock Creek cab ride, we're hurtling down a road we can't quite see. Even worse, we're not quite sure who is driving the car—but we know it isn't us, and we worry that no one may be.

---

36 Eric Ravenscraft, "How to Make Your Phone Limit Your Screen Time For You" *New York Times*, April 1, 2019.

CHAPTER 2

Our Brains, Prosperity, and Emergent Order

———

To the naïve mind that can conceive of order only as the product of deliberate arrangement, it may seem absurd that in complex conditions order, and adaptation to the unknown, can be achieved more effectively by decentralizing decisions and that a division of authority will actually extend the possibility of overall order.[37]

— FREDERICH HAYEK

Maybe the way to deal with the complexity of the world is to get away, separate oneself from it, simplify aggressively, and get more parts of your life directly under your control rather than relying on others?

---

37 Friedrich Hayek, *The Fatal Conceit*, (Chicago, University of Chicago Press, 1988).

In April 2018, I took a week off after wrapping up my duties as acting Chief Technologist at the Federal Trade Commission and before starting my new job at the Charles Koch Institute. That week was the first time I could remember that I had no job duties hanging over my head. Nothing! I decided to use that time to disconnect, relax, reset, and reconnect with nature. So, I drove to Lake Moomaw, in the middle of nowhere in western Virginia. This man-made lake, created by damming the Jackson River that flows through George Washington National Forest, has forty-three miles of uninterrupted forested shoreline. I paddled a loaded canoe a mile out into the lake to a decent shore-side site on a narrow peninsula and set up camp at least two hours from any type of mobile reception. I pitched my tent, gathered a little firewood near the stone fire ring someone had made, had some dinner, and watched the sun set. Four days without communicating with another human. Relaxation time was here.

And then it started raining. In the quiet woods and with the open lake next to me, I could hear the rain coming nearly thirty minutes before it hit my camp. I suspended a large tarp over a good portion of my camp, added to my firewood pile, poured myself a finger of bourbon, and hunkered down.

For the next two and a half days I spent most of my time adjusting the tarp to block the continuous wind and rain from my gear while allowing smoke from my fire to escape. As the days wore on, I climbed further and further up the steep hill behind my tent looking for firewood, and I wore a path through the brush shuttling food back and forth from the bear bag I had suspended in a tree fifty meters away.

I really enjoy camping. But this was not relaxing.

Yet somehow hiding under a tarp all day also got a little boring. I had failed to download any music to my phone, but I had an audiobook: *The Martian* by Andy Weir. If you recall the premise of the book (or the faithful-to-the-book movie starring Matt Damon), the main character, Mark Watney, is left alone in the harshest of climates on the red planet with only his wits and a few meager resources to keep himself alive. External speaker strapped to my belt, I listened to Mark as he "worked the problem" to survive. I felt like his earthbound analogue, although admittedly western Virginia is somewhat less remote than Mars and I faced far fewer life-threatening incidents.

I do remember one dicey moment of that trip, however. It was twilight and I had yet again hiked up the hill, hunting semi-dry wood to tide me over for the night. Swinging my hatchet at the latest semi-soggy branch I deemed fire-worthy, my foot slipped. The hatchet's momentum carried it past the branch, and it glanced off my shin. The blade didn't connect with my leg, but I kept wondering what I would have done if it had. Would I have been able to bandage the wound? Would I have had to canoe in the pouring rain and gusting wind back to my car? And then what? (I cannot convey how much my wife hates this story, by the way.) It wasn't as dramatic as Mark blowing out an airlock on Mars and nearly dying from decompression, but it was a stark reminder that I was alone.

On the fourth day the storm finally subsided, and I did get a chance to sit in the sun and read and fish for some time before breaking camp and paddling back to my car. I remember getting actual chills from the first pop song I heard on the radio. A mere four days without any music was enough to make any random song sound as emotionally compelling as Wagner.

Those four days were my closest recent experience to the "self-sufficient" lifestyle many of us (including me) sometimes romanticize. For those four days, I partially removed myself from the intricate emergent order that is our modern economy and society. I simplified my life. I was "in control" in a way that I usually am not, day-to-day. I built my own shelter, gathered my own heating supplies, set my own schedule, and prepared my own food.

I wasn't fully disconnected from society, of course: I benefited from modern fabrics, foodstuffs, equipment, and entertainment that I certainly could not have created by myself. But even with these advantages, I spent a lot of time and energy in manual labor. For four days, that was fine; it was the point, even. But a life lived that way would be a constant struggle.

Driving back into society, I did not feel relaxed, refreshed, or reconnected to nature. If anything, I felt slightly resentful toward nature. Yet the trip was an enormous success as a reminder of how poor is the person who depends only on themselves. I was reminded how intertwined with others' my life normally is and how much richer it is because of those connections. I left those woods grateful for the complexity of the world I had temporarily escaped.

As discussed in the previous chapter, the complexity, interconnectedness, and emergent order of the modern world can make the world feel like it is out of control. But those connections we have with others enrich us intellectually, socially, and materially.

This chapter is about how the deeply entwined and interconnected nature of modern society emerged over time. When humans moved from hunter-gatherer to agriculture, we augmented our bodies and brains. Most of these augments—complex systems like cities, governments, and social norms—emerged in conjunction with the transition to agriculture and evolved slowly over several millennia. But about 250 years ago, the evolution of many of these systems jumped to warp speed. The dramatic widespread increase in prosperity during the modern period has occurred because our augments have become so much more complex, interconnected, and influenced by all of us, but out of any one person's control.

OUR AMAZING AND LIMITED BRAINS

To grasp the complexity of modern society, let's start with society's fundamental building block: the human brain. Our brains are immensely complicated and extremely powerful. In the introduction I noted that our bodies are emergent systems. This is also true of the brain. There is no single human brain cell that commands the other cells. Instead, the connections between the cells power the brain, with each cell influencing and being influenced by many other cells. This is true across the animal kingdom. But human brains are particularly interesting. As far as we can tell, humans are the only species with the capacity to think deeply about what we are thinking.[38] In other words, you are an emergent system that has become conscious of your ability to think.

The average adult human brain is a gel-like, soft tofu consistency, weighs two-and-a-half to three pounds, and is about the size of a large grapefruit or a cantaloupe.[39] Neuroscientists estimate that there are around one hundred billion neurons in your brain—about the same as the number of stars in the Milky Way.[40] These neurons have an estimated 100 trillion connections between them, composed of five hundred thousand miles of nerve fibers.[41]

Those three pounds of complex tofu make you who you are. The mind-brain connection is philosophically and physiologically complicated, but few doubt that human consciousness is related to that bundle of grey matter. And our individual brains are shaped by—and learn from—the experiences we encounter throughout our lives. We aren't replicas of each other or even of our parents. The emergent nature of our brains means we each are unique.

The computational power of the human brain is tremendous. My one-year-old daughter's brain can recognize images with a fidelity that surpasses that of the most powerful supercomputers. And the brain is remarkably efficient. As Stanford professor of neurobiology Liqun Luo explains,

38 Stanford Encyclopedia of Philosophy, "Self-Consciousness," accessed March 30, 2021.
39 "How does the brain work?," NCBI, accessed February 10, 2021., Eric Jensen, *Teaching with the Brain in Mind*, (ASCD, 2005).
40 Sarah DeWeerdt, "How to map the brain," *Nature*, July 24, 2019.
41 "Transmitting fibers in the brain: Total length and distribution of lengths," *AI Impacts*, accessed February 10, 2021.

"[A] professional tennis player can follow the trajectory of a tennis ball after it is served at a speed as high as 160 miles per hour, move to the optimal spot on the court, position his or her arm, and swing the racket to return the ball in the opponent's court, all within a few hundred milliseconds. Moreover, the brain can accomplish all these tasks (with the help of the body it controls) with power consumption about tenfold less than a personal computer."[42]

But the brain isn't just good at physical and perceptual tasks. As a learning and thinking device, it is without parallel. Scientists estimate that the brain can hold around two petabytes of information—approximately the entire contents of the Library of Congress.[43] Children usually learn complex cognitive skills such as speech, reasoning, and imagination without any kind of formal instruction. The entirety of human knowledge and achievement, from Shakespeare to Feynman, is a direct result of computation in human brains.

All of this works even though the brain is a twenty-watt machine composed of heavily connected but relatively simple cells that are constantly dying off.

But our complex and emergent brains have clear limits. Many of these limits are inherent in the physical structure of the brain. They are a result of an organ that has developed to serve certain specific purposes and out of efficiency has not

---

42   Liqun Luo, "Why Is the Human Brain So Efficient?," *Nautilus*, April 12, 2018.

43   Tia Ghose, "The Human Brain's Memory Could Store the Entire Internet," *LiveScience*, February 18, 2016.

developed to serve other purposes. For example, our memory stores strong experiences; we forget most everything else. There are obviously limits to what knowledge we can successfully master in a tight time frame. We remember strange, often useless material. And we forget. Oh boy, do we forget. I can still remember my childhood phone number that I haven't used in twenty years, but regularly forget the name of the person I just met.

We also have a wide range of cognitive biases. These biases are preconceived ideas or tendencies that our brains use as shortcuts to quickly deal with complex information. They are systematic mismatches between the world around us and our brain's model of that world. Some commonly described biases include:

- **Anchoring Bias**: This involves people's tendency to overly rely on the first piece of information they encounter to make future decisions. This can occur in salary negotiations, for example, where an individual will use a stated offer to negotiate for a raise.
- **Bandwagon Effect**: This involves a type of "group think" where an individual will choose to engage in an activity or support a position because most other individuals show similar behavior.
- **Confirmation Bias**: This occurs when an individual chooses to see unrelated events as supporting his or her preconceived notions or ideas. For example, knowing that someone comes from a particular socioeconomic background may cause individuals to interpret that person's behavior as reflective of their upbringing.

- **Conservatism Bias:** This involves an overwhelming belief in old or outdated information, even when new evidence indicates that this information is likely incorrect. People's belief in the flatness of the world despite evidence suggesting that it is round constitutes an example of conservatism bias.
- **Recency Bias:** This involves individuals' tendency to rely on the latest information and ignore older or historical data. Sell-offs in the stock market exemplify the recency bias as individuals base their decisions on prices at the moment and ignore the historical upward trends of the market.

The term "bias" has negative connotations, but these biases are simply tools our brains have developed that work well in some situations but not others. Scientists are unsure to what degree such biases are a result of the physical characteristics of the brain or the "software" that runs on that hardware, or both. Either way, our biases help us solve problems. Author and startup founder Buster Benson has described four problems that biases help us solve: 1) too much information; 2) not enough meaning; 3) a need to act quickly; and 4) choosing what to remember.[44] These are important problems to solve, and cognitive biases can save us time and energy. But like many shortcuts, they do have tradeoffs.

Our brains' limits obviously affect our lives. For example, British anthropologist Robin Dunbar has estimated that our brain can only maintain about 150 productive social

---

44 Buster Benson, "Cognitive bias cheat sheet: Because thinking is hard," *Better Humans*, accessed March 1, 2021.

relationships. This so-called "Dunbar number" shapes the organizations of human communities, workplaces, and even online social communities.[45]

The capabilities of our brains and their limits are the results of adaptation to our environment over time. The physical structures of our species' brains evolved over time to adapt to the conditions our predecessors encountered. But we, as humans, can think about how we think. That means we can overcome our cognitive biases and other mental limits. We can augment our brains.

HOW WE AUGMENT OUR BRAINS

"Shut up, brain! I don't need you now, I have friends!"

— LISA SIMPSON

On an evolutionary timescale, our brains and bodies are largely identical to those of our ancestors a thousand years ago. Even a few thousand years are not enough for significant evolutionary changes. If an infant from the seventeenth century were dropped into a family in the twentieth century, she'd grow up just like any other kid. Three hundred years is the blink of an eye in the evolutionary timescale.

Yet an adult from the seventeenth century wouldn't recognize our everyday experience of being a human in 2021. Not only

---

45   Christine Ro, "Dunbar's number: Why we can only maintain 150 relationships," *BBC Future*, October 9, 2019.

would the most basic technologies of today be fantastical to such a visitor, how we address our fundamental needs would also be completely foreign. Today, most people—unless they are camping—spend only a fraction of their time directly pursuing basic physical needs such as food and shelter. Instead, we work at highly specialized tasks for which we are compensated—and then we trade that compensation for our material needs. Imagine explaining an ATM to a seventeenth-century serf.

A seventeenth-century farmer would be bewildered in our world today because so much has changed. But if this change isn't a result of our more evolved brains, what did cause it? How did humans transition away from hunter-gatherer culture without evolutionary changes? More recently, how did we transition into the enormous prosperity of the last two and a half centuries?

While our brains remain physically well-suited to tribal life, humankind has figured out how to move beyond the limits of our individual brains. Yes, our brains evolved for small, tribal associations over millions of years. But humankind stepped out of that evolutionary condition about eight to ten thousand years ago when many humans moved from hunter-gatherer societies to agricultural societies.[46] To a far greater degree than any other species, we became specialists at augmenting ourselves, including our brains, through tools.

Most people can intuitively understand how new *physical* tools augmented and enhanced human *physical* abilities. From

---

46 Graeme Barker, *The Agricultural Revolution in Prehistory: Why did Foragers become Farmers?*, (Oxford University Press, 2005).

primitive tools like axes and blades to modern agricultural combines, these simple and eventually more complex physical objects have magnified human physical labor. For example, the basic steam engine, used in everything from factories to locomotives, placed massive amounts of physical force under the direction of a single human.

We also developed many tools to magnify our cognitive abilities. Most of the "tools" that we have developed to augment our limited brainpower are not designed or engineered like a plow or steam engine, however. They are emergent phenomena, developed by millions and billions of people through usage, experimentation, and feedback.

Language, for example, "is an emergent system par excellence."[47] Language is learned from other humans and evolves through usage over time. No single person defines language. We determine it together in a complex process of usage and feedback. Even the way children learn language is emergent. They don't memorize specific words, but instead extract patterns from repeated exposure to spoken words. This enables them to, even early on, recombine patterns they've heard into novel patterns they have never heard.

Even something as tangible and seemingly static as writing is emergent. Writing is a highly useful mental augment that allows us to store a record of our thoughts for later use by ourselves or others. But, like spoken language, written language isn't designed by any one person or group. Font

---

47   K. David Harrison and E. Raimy, "Language As An Emergent System," *Soundings*, 90 no. 1/2, (2007).

designers may create new ways to represent individual letters, but they do not dictate how those letters are arranged—and they themselves are building upon an ancient tradition of how letters are shaped. After all, a font of unrecognizable shapes will not be useful to most people trying to write.

The limits of our brains have not held humanity back. We are the best species by far at developing tools that augment our limited brains. Language, whether written or spoken, is just one of the many mental augments humans have developed in an emergent manner. Others include societal institutions such as the family, tribe, and government, all of which amplify our ability to defend ourselves and provide for ourselves.

Other important emergent phenomena include our ethical beliefs and values. These ideas shape individual actions. Economic historian Deirdre McCloskey has argued persuasively and lyrically that it was the changed beliefs of individuals and society to certain "bourgeois values" that drove the growth of the modern world. Specifically, after eons of deep skepticism of innovation and those who attempt it, societies in certain regions began to tolerate and even praise those who sought to make things better, including those who did so through commerce and trade.[48] Like the other tools we've discussed, these beliefs and their application were not the product of any one mind, but were the result of the actions of multitudes.

One of the primary ways we augment our minds is by specialization, division of labor, and trade. Any random

---

48 Deirdre Nansen McCloskey, *Bourgeois Equality: How Ideas, Not Capital or Institutions, Enriched the World*, (University of Chicago Press, 2016).

seventeenth-century individual was highly likely to be involved in agriculture to meet their own family's needs. Today the average American farmer grows enough food to feed three hundred people.[49] It used to be common to make one's clothes; as a result, few people had more than one or two changes of clothes. Today, few people—even among the poorest people in the world—make their own clothes, and most who do so do it as a hobby, not a necessity. Rather than trying to meet all our needs ourselves, work is divided up into very narrow specializations and we trade with each other to meet our needs and desires. For example, I specialize in understanding tech policy. I trade that expertise for money with which I can purchase the results of other people's expertise, including food, shelter, and clothing.

This specialization enables expertise, focus, and investment, raising total output. It also means we are bound to and reliant on others. And we rarely know these other people at all.

THESE EMERGENT AUGMENTS HAVE CREATED EMERGENT ORDER

Many of these tools have greatly expanded our ability to accomplish ever more complex things as a species. Indeed, humans keep getting better at tool building, and our tools keep becoming more complex. Today, the most powerful systems in which humans participate are too complex to have one person in charge. They produce value through emergent

---

49 Deirdre Nansen McCloskey, *Bourgeois Equality: How Ideas, Not Capital or Institutions, Enriched the World*, (University of Chicago Press, 2016,) 7.

order. And even simple-seeming systems are far more complex than we realize.

Human life is more than the economy, but the economy provides a good example of the modern world's reliance on complex emergent order. Leonard E. Read wrote an excellent essay called "I, Pencil" that demonstrates this complexity.[50] The essay, written in first person from the perspective of a simple yellow #2 pencil, proves that "not a single person on the face of this earth knows how to make" such a pencil: a simple pencil consisting of "wood, lacquer, the printed labeling, graphite lead, a bit of metal, and an eraser."[51] Yet each of these elements required the work of loggers, miners, forgers, and many more. Considering just the wood of the pencil, Read writes:

"My family tree begins with what in fact is a tree, a cedar of straight grain that grows in Northern California and Oregon. Now contemplate all the saws and trucks and rope and the countless other gear used in harvesting and carting the cedar logs to the railroad siding. Think of all the persons and the numberless skills that went into their fabrication: the mining of ore, the making of steel and its refinement into saws, axes, motors; the growing of hemp and bringing it through all the stages to heavy and strong rope; the logging camps with their beds and mess halls, the cookery and the raising of all the foods. Why, untold thousands of persons had a hand in every cup of coffee the loggers drink!"[52]

---

50 Leonard Reed, "I, Pencil," *FEE*, March 3, 2015.
51 Ibid. 4.
52 Ibid. 4.

Similarly, Read describes how the pencil's "lead" is graphite from Sri Lanka mixed with clay from Mississippi and wax from Mexico, among other things. He points out the castor-bean-based lacquer, the zinc and copper metal end, and the many international ingredients appearing in the deceptively simple eraser.[53] A single yellow number #2 pencil requires the collaboration of millions of people, each of whom contributes only "a tiny, infinitesimal bit of know-how" to the total process.[54] Most of these specialized workers have no idea they are helping to make pencils.

The most amazing thing about this complex web of processes is that it is not static. It can and does adjust constantly to changing circumstances. If cedar prices rise because of a shortage, the pencil manufacturer will look for adequate substitutes or perhaps pay the increased price and look for savings elsewhere. Changes in demand or supply for the many material and labor components of the pencil will ripple through the economy as millions of people choose how or whether to adjust their decisions based on new information. These decisions reallocate resources across the many different products that compete for those materials and labor. No one is in charge of this interconnected process. The price change of pencils due to a cedar shortage is a result of the actions of millions. It emerges.

And that's just a simple pencil. Imagine the difficulty of detailing even a fraction of the many contributors to a complex piece of machinery like a Boeing 747 or an iPhone. And

---

53 Ibid. 5.
54 Leonard Read, "I, Pencil," *FEE*, March 3, 2015: 7.

then multiply that by all the millions of products—"simple" or complex—and services that are created, distributed, bought, and used every day.

No one can understand this process in detail. When it works—which is the overwhelming amount of the time—it is practically invisible. We don't think about what it took to produce that pencil we just jotted a note with and which we bought in a six-pack for a couple of bucks from Walgreens. We take for granted that grocery stores will have stocked shelves, even though each and every product on those shelves is the result of a combined effort by thousands of individuals.

Because it works so well, we are surprised when something breaks down. Everyone recently experienced one particularly personal breakdown: the Great Coronavirus Toilet Paper Shortage. For several weeks starting in March of 2020, it became very difficult to locate toilet paper in US retail stores.[55] Amazon had shortages and long delivery times.[56] I remember logging in and seeing only industrial sizes of toilet paper that I wasn't sure how we would use in our household.

The cause of this shortage was skyrocketing consumer demand. This demand was driven in part by panic buying but also because consumers were using so much more toilet paper at home.

---

55   Michael Corkery and Sapna Maheshwari, "Is There Really a Toilet Paper Shortage," *The New York Times*, March 13, 2020.

56   Annie Palmer, "Why ordering from Amazon has been so unpredictable during the coronavirus crisis," *CNBC*, May 9, 2020.

It turns out that there are two very separate supply chains for toilet paper: one commercial and one consumer-facing. As people stayed home, they shifted demand from the commercial supply chain to the consumer one. Toilet paper manufacturer Georgia-Pacific (owner of brands Angel Soft and Quilted Northern) estimated that the average household would use 40 percent more toilet paper if everyone stayed home.[57] So as people retreated home from their workplaces, there was a shortage in the consumer supply chain. But as workplaces closed, there was a glut in the commercial toilet paper supply chain—which is why you saw some creative restaurants offer free rolls of toilet paper with takeout food.

Something as seemingly simple as toilet paper can be at the center of a complex problem. The same complexity that delivers prosperity also means that such problems don't have simple, single solutions. No one person decreed how consumer and commercial toilet paper should be allocated. No one had sufficient knowledge to evaluate how important toilet paper is to each person compared to the other resources they might be seeking. Instead, the shortage subsided as manufacturers, distributors, retailers, and customers all changed their practices in an interrelated set of decisions by millions of people. In other words, the process of complex feedback through prices and purchasing behavior redistributed resources in a way that met the new levels of demand—not because any one person solved the whole problem, but because millions of people each solved the specific problem they faced.

---

57 "Statement on Georgia-Pacific's Response to COVID-19," Georgia Pacific, accessed February 10, 2021.

EMERGENT ORDER IN THE ECONOMY HAS GENERATED UNPRECEDENTED WEALTH

"The question isn't why are some people poor. Poverty is the state of nature. The question is how did some become wealthy."

— PER BYLUND

Complex systems of emergent order can make us feel like we are out of control, but in the economy, such systems have generated unprecedented wealth and human well-being. For most of human history, the average human lived on less than three dollars' worth of materials a day. In the last two hundred years or so, wealth creation has accelerated exponentially. Today, it is closer to thirty dollars per day on average, and in more developed countries it is over one hundred dollars per day. If you graph the incredible modern spread of human wealth and well-being, you get an exponential growth curve, or what economist Don Boudreaux calls the "hockey stick of human prosperity."[58]

Economic historian Deirdre McCloskey calls this "The Great Enrichment."[59] As McCloskey notes, earth is not a paradise; too many people remain poor "in nations of economic hell."[60] But "until 1800, though, such hell was what everybody except a handful of nobles and priests and merchants expected, year

---

58 *MR University*, "The Hockey Stick of Human Prosperity" March 13, 2019. video, 4:54.

59 Deirdre Nansen McCloskey, *Bourgeois Equality: How Ideas, Not Capital or Institutions, Enriched the World*, (University of Chicago Press, 2016), 5.

60 Ibid.

after terrible year."[61] Today, the *average* ordinary human, instead of hell, has "a pretty good purgatory."[62] As the site HumanProgress.org characterizes it, "Between 1800 and 1900, GDP per person per day doubled. In other words, income grew over twice as much in one century as it had over the preceding 18 combined."[63] The same article further explains that:

- In 1820, around 90 percent of the world lived in extreme poverty while less than 10 percent of the current population lives in similar conditions.
- From 1800 to 2016, unskilled laborers' hourly wages increased by an estimated 31,627 percent while hourly wages for production workers grew by 79,775 percent.
- While most individuals in Europe and the Americas would live until their mid-30s during the 1870s, they currently possess a life expectancy anywhere between seventy-two to eighty-one years.
- Over the same time periods, illiteracy, child mortality rates, and death from conflicts decreased dramatically, while food supply and democratic governments increased.[64]

The benefits of our complex emergent orders are widespread demographically and geographically, unprecedented in human history, and go far beyond mere economic enrichment to benefits that include longer, healthier, more educated, and enjoyable lives.

---

61   Ibid.
62   Ibid.
63   Marian Tupy, "The Great Miracle of Industrialization," *Human Progress*, May 6, 2019.
64   Ibid.

CONCLUSION

Today, we live in a world where we are so rich that a shortage of toilet paper is a problem worthy of news coverage. We have augmented our powerful but limited brains so successfully that what would have been an incredibly expensive luxury good two hundred years ago is now seen as a necessity, a shortage of which raises panic.

Our incredibly complex problem-solving systems guide the decisions of millions without any central control, driving the widespread growth in material prosperity that has benefited humankind for the past two centuries. Our modern lives rely on complex systems of emergent order in which we all participate but none of us controls.

This emergent order has made clear that we are not in control, but it has also made us incredibly rich. Abandoning this enriching complexity isn't a viable option. If you don't believe me, go solo camping in the middle of nowhere for a few days.

And then imagine an entire world of solo campers. It would be a world of independent, self-reliant, and impoverished people.

Rather than abandon emergent order and its benefits, we should use our uniquely powerful brains to better understand it and how it drives this complexity and prosperity.

CHAPTER 3

What is Emergent Order?

———

"To see complex systems of functional order as order, and not as chaos, takes understanding. The leaves drooping from the trees in autumn, the interior of an airplane engine, the entrails of a rabbit, the city desk of a newspaper, all appear to be chaos if they are seen without comprehension. Once they are seen as systems of order, they actually look different."

— JANE JACOBS[65]

I'm sitting in the upstairs bedroom of my brother's house in a small neighborhood in mostly rural southern Pennsylvania. It's a typical new-ish housing development, with lots and houses that are much bigger than the upstate NY suburbs he and I grew up in. My wife, daughter, and I live in DC, but we are riding out the COVID-19 pandemic here to take advantage of the space and to split childcare duties more

---

65   James C. Scott, *Seeing Like A State*, (Yale University Press, 1998), 133.

broadly. My favorite spot to write is in the upstairs bedroom, desk directly facing a window.

The view out of my window is order and complexity. The windowpane slices the world outside into a three-by-four grid. Number the squares one through twelve from the top left. What could be more orderly? Yet the contents of each square are a view into a world of complexity. Panes one, two, three, five, and six contain only cloudy sky, as uniform as the gray-painted wall of some industrial building. Panes seven and eight in the middle left frame the cul de sac on which my brother's house sits. This paved teardrop was designed and built, as was the neighbor's house that occupies panes seven and four.

Panes seven and eight also contain the neighbor's front yard. The groomed bushes and trees around the house were chosen and planted, again according to a plan. But what about the bushes and trees themselves? They had no architect, yet they grow and branch in complex but orderly ways—even though no central control governs their growth. The lawn is trimmed with geometric precision, but it also grows without central order or control. The platoon of rabbits that occasionally marches across panes seven through twelve are not designed, but still orderly—and cute. (And what patterns might emerge from observing their population changes over time?)[66]

In fact, just eyeballing it, I'd estimate that more than six panes—more than half of this suburban view—is filled with

---

66 *See* Melanie Mitchell, *Complexity: A Guided Tour*, (Oxford University Press, 2009), 22-34 (discussing the population of rabbits as background to a simple formula known as a logistical map that has surprising properties).

plants, animals, or other entities that are orderly but not designed. They exhibit emergent order.

DEFINING EMERGENT ORDER

What do I mean when I say, "emergent order"? The term is abstract and interconnected with many other related concepts. But let's start with a similarly abstract definition and then clarify further with examples.

Emergent order is the <u>complex behavior</u> of a <u>system</u> created by the interactions of <u>many smaller components</u> following <u>simpler rules</u> with <u>no central control</u>.

Let's dig into the underlined terms in that definition using a classic example of emergent order, an ant colony.

- There is a <u>system</u> made up of <u>many smaller interacting parts</u>. The ant colony is the system; the individual ants are the many smaller parts.
- The system exhibits <u>complex behavior</u>. "Complex" is relative to the simplicity of the smaller parts. Complex behavior is more than the sum of its parts. It is organized but hard to predict. For example, ant colonies can build elaborate nests. They can place graveyards for dead ants with near mathematical precision equidistant from the main colony and the colony's junkyard. They can find and move large pieces of food long distances. Certain types of ant colonies can evacuate an anthill and march to a new location, building complex structures out of individual ants in order to traverse hazards.

- The smaller components follow simpler rules. The behavior of an individual drone ant is much simpler than the complex behavior of the entire colony. For example, ants foraging for food appear to wander aimlessly, but leave pheromones that other ants can sense. When an ant finds food, it returns to the hill, strengthening the pheromone trail. Each ant that comes upon that trail and follows it also strengthens that trail. The cumulative result is, over time, a highway of pheromones lighting a trail to the food source. When the food source runs out, the pheromones fade as fewer ants walk along the pathway. The end result is a sophisticated, complex effort, but each individual ant follows simple rules.
- There is no central control. Most ant colonies have queens, but the queen does not command or lead an ant colony. There is no hierarchy in how ant colonies make decisions.[67] It is somewhat strange to even call them "decisions" because even though no individual ant makes the decision for the colony, the decision occurs at the colony level—it *emerges* from the actions of the many individual ants.

Emergent order is common in biological systems, but it occurs in many other types of systems. Let's look at another example—this time involving humans—and use that example to compare and contrast **emergent order** with **randomness** and with **designed order**.

You've probably been to a sporting event where the crowd at some point did "the wave." This aptly named group

---

67 Steve Johnson, *Emergence: The Connected Lives of Ants, Brains, Cities, and Software* (Scribner, August 28, 2001).

performance has people standing and sitting in coordination to form a visual wave pattern that travels around the stadium. The wave exhibits classic characteristics of emergent order. The system is the attendees at the sporting event. The complex behavior is the coordinated, observable pattern of a wave moving around a stadium. It is more complicated than the behavior of the individuals. The components are individual sports fans. No one controls the action of the wave. And the simple rules are something approximating "stand when those near you stand and sit after a little bit." Each individual participant judges whether and when to stand, based on their own internal state (Am I excited? Am I tired? Am I rooting for the home team or not?) and on the actions of others around them (Are many others participating? Is the wave "coming"? Is it "passed"?). Even though the individual decision is simple in its output (stand or sit), the inputs that each person considers are many, and the result is the complex coordination of many people to produce an orderly result. This is emergent order.

It's also interesting to think about how this process starts and stops. In many cases the wave starts with a small group of dedicated individuals who attempt to persuade, by their own coordinated action, everyone else to participate. In order to succeed, other individuals have to be in the mood to participate. As the number of participants grows, so does the peer pressure to also participate. This positive feedback means that less enthusiastic individuals get swept up into participating as more and more people around them join. The success of a wave effort reflects something about the energy of the crowd, while also generating enthusiasm in the crowd, which is why it is such a popular technique. Starting the wave feels like a sign of approval from thousands of people; participating feels like you are part of something bigger than yourself; and we have all experienced the awkwardness of watching an enthusiastic person who tries to start the wave and cannot get a critical mass to agree.

Note that the instigating group does not control the wave. Indeed, once the wave picks up speed, the instigators become regular participants, keeping the wave alive by following the same rough intuition that everyone else is using about when to stand or when to sit.

This lack of anyone in control is particularly clear when we look at how waves end. They can peter out or can collapse rather rapidly, with more and more people feeling that they have participated long enough or that something interesting is happening in the game. Their own refusal to stand conveys to others nearby that it might be time to stop. This negative feedback (negative because it reduces participation in the phenomenon) can spread rapidly, dissolving the emergent phenomenon despite no one individual commanding everyone to stop.

Compare the emergent order of the wave to random crowd action. Take that same stadium crowd and watch it filter into the stadium before a game begins. During the wave, you could probably guess relatively accurately when a specific fan might sit or stand. The pattern is identifiable. But as fans enter the stadium, you would probably be hard pressed to predict when any particular fan would arrive and take their seat. There is little obvious order to how a stadium fills with fans, other than that it tends to fill up toward the start time of the game. There are smaller components acting without central control, but the system exhibits no complex behavior; it barely seems like a system at all. This action is unordered, or <u>random</u>.

Finally, imagine the college football game where the home team fans have been given placards that, when everyone holds them up, spell out "GO TEAM" across the entire stadium. This is not random; the system of smaller components exhibits a complex behavior that is very orderly. But that order is centrally designed. Someone plotted out the exact location for each placard and coordinated the display. It does not emerge from individual behavior; each individual is given directives that, taken together, create the intended result. This is <u>designed order</u>.

MORE EXAMPLES OF EMERGENT ORDER

Emergent order is common in crowd behavior. Think about standing ovations or calls for an encore at a musical event. Less positively, riots are emergent. Instigating individuals act out, spurring others nearby to take an action they otherwise wouldn't have. This can spread rapidly through an angry crowd.

I've often thought particularly about emergent phenomena in the context of dancing at concerts. Washington, DC, where I live, is somewhat notorious for concertgoers who stand and bop their heads but do very little else. This is particularly true in larger venues where the "signal" of one person dancing can dissipate quickly in a crowd of uptight urban professionals. But take the exact same people and same music, cram them into a small venue, and the result could be much more active dancing because the signals of a few enthusiastic dancers are more easily conveyed to other concertgoers.

Crowd behaviors are one example of a broader subset of emergent order: social norms. Psychologist and researcher Michele Gelfand defines social norms as "socially agreed-upon standards of behavior."[68] Table manners are one type of social norm; so is being quiet in a movie theater, making eye contact when speaking to someone, and greeting people with a handshake or a kiss. Most social norms are so ingrained that we barely know we are participating in them. Despite this ubiquity, Gelfand explains that "social norms are the building blocks of social order; without them, society would crumble."[69] Social norms help us predict what other people will do. They help us coordinate with millions of others who share the same basic norms and can create conflict with people who do not share our basic views.

Other examples of emergent order abound. As I mentioned in the introduction, your body is an emergent system. Individual cells of your body each follow their programming. The emergent result, which no single cell governs or controls, is the stable macro-level pattern known as your body. It's made up of cells, but as a whole your body does much more than what is contained in the programming of those cells.

The classic economic example of emergent order is the price system. In a free market economy, the price for any one

---

68   Michele Gefland, *Rule Makers, Rule Breakers* (Simon & Schuster, 2018), 7.
69   Ibid. 17.

product or service is the result of a complex web of information that no one controls. A shopkeeper selling canned peaches makes an educated guess on the proper price for a can of peaches based on their local knowledge of what the can of peaches cost them to purchase and display, as well as their knowledge of what the shop's customers are willing to pay. That local knowledge is summarized in the shopkeeper's price for a can of peaches—just as the price charged to the shopkeeper captured the costs of farming the peaches and mining the aluminum to make the can and the salary for the graphic designer who created the label, among many other factors. Similarly, if Andy's pie shop buys canned peaches to make peach pie, the price of Andy's pie will incorporate the information conveyed by the shopkeeper's price, plus his own contribution of local knowledge. If the price of aluminum rises, peaches might become more expensive, and Andy might have to increase the price of his pies—but he need not know that is why the price of peaches has increased. Prices emerge as a result of millions of individual decisions about how to use limited resources.

CHARACTERISTICS OF SYSTEMS EXHIBITING EMERGENCE

Social norms, biology, and economics are just a few areas where systems generate emergent order. Not all systems exhibit emergent order, and those that do share some common characteristics. Systems with these characteristics are called *complex systems.* Indeed, many experts in what I am calling emergent order would describe themselves as experts in complex systems. Emergent order is a property of complex systems. In fact, one of the leading experts in complex systems, Dr. Melanie

Mitchell, offers one simplified definition of complexity (there is no standardized definition): "a system that exhibits non-trivial emergent and self-organizing behaviors."[70]

"Complexity" refers in part to the range of potential behaviors that a system could exhibit. A more complex system typically has a wider range of potential behaviors. When individual ants move decaying material around their nest, the resulting moderation of the nest's temperature is an emergent behavior of the colony. But an ant colony is *complex* because it can exhibit that and many other sophisticated behaviors as the result of relatively simple behaviors by individual ants.

The study of complex systems is a vast and complicated area of inquiry I cannot fully summarize for you—I'll admit, I cannot fully follow every thread myself. I highly recommend Dr. Melanie Mitchell's book *Complexity: A Guided Tour* for a more thorough exploration.

With that caveat, let's explore some of the common, somewhat overlapping and intertwined, themes of complex systems and how they connect to emergent order. I hope to build a more complete image of emergent order, but I have no illusions that I'll capture every nuance in the discussion below. This is a deep and rich subject and if I can just give you a flavor for it that makes you hungry for more, I will have accomplished my goal.

---

70 Melanie Mitchell, Complexity: A Guided Tour, (Oxford University Press, 2009), 13.

ANTI-REDUCTIONISM: THE WHOLE IS MORE THAN THE SUM OF ITS PARTS

A classic approach to understanding something is to conceptually (or sometimes physically) break it into its pieces, understand the pieces, and then assemble this understanding until you understand the whole. This *reductionism* has been the primary approach to scientific understanding for centuries.[71] Reductionism especially dominated physics, where it had great success at describing large-scale phenomena such as how the planets move and very small-scale phenomena such as how atoms interact. Reductionists hoped that all phenomena could be understood by understanding atoms and then working their way up from there. But this dream hasn't worked out for many "human-scale" phenomena, as Mitchell puts it. Even though we're all made up of atoms, understanding the physics of atoms does not tell us much about the weather, living organisms, or economies, for example. As she explains,

> *"The anti-reductionist catch phrase, 'the whole is more than the sum of its parts,' takes on increasing significance as new sciences such as chaos, systems biology, evolutionary economics, and network theory move beyond reductionism to explain how complex behavior can arise from large collections of simpler components."*[72]

Many systems are complicated. A car engine, for example, is a complicated assembly of many smaller parts that all work together to power an automobile. But if we wanted to model the output of a car engine, we could do so by measuring

---

71 Ibid. 9.
72 Ibid. 10.

the inputs of gasoline and oxygen and the resulting output RPM and torque. The details of the specific parts wouldn't matter to the accuracy of the model. The operation of the engine could be reduced to a few simple equations. Similarly, the solar system is very complicated—many details are involved, including you and me. But when it comes to predicting the orbits of the planets over time, all those details can be ignored. Relatively simple equations can be used to calculate the planets' paths.

But complex systems cannot be reduced like this. The behavior of the system is fundamentally different from and more sophisticated than the behaviors of the individual elements. The smaller components and how they interact are essential to the order that emerges. This means, for example, that even if you understood everything about an individual ant and how it would behave in various situations, you would not be able to predict the behavior of the entire colony. The behavior of the whole emerges from the interactions between the parts. The equations that would accurately model such a system would have to be as complicated as the system itself. This means the system cannot be accurately simplified—the only way to accurately model the system is to run it.

As Kevin Kelly poetically puts it: "[T]here is nothing to be found in a beehive that is not submerged in a bee. And yet you can search a bee forever with cyclotron and fluoroscope, and you will never find the hive."[73]

---

73   Kevin Kelly, *Out of Control: The New Biology of Machines, Social Systems, & the Economic World,* (Basic Books, 1992), 283.

BOUNDARIES, SIGNALS, AND HIERARCHIES

Describing an emergent system as one where the *whole* is more than the sum of its *parts* smuggles into the discussion three concepts that we need to unpack to understand emergent order: boundaries, hierarchies, and signals.[74]

A **boundary** is the physical or conceptual edge of system. Boundaries separate one thing from another. A fence, for example, separates Bob's property from Tom's property. In complex systems, a boundary separates one system from another. In an ant colony, one type of boundary is the exoskeleton of an ant. In a software system, a subroutine or an application programming interface form a boundary. In an economy, legal and practical boundaries separate one company from another. Boundaries are porous, but not indiscriminately so. Think again of a fence but with a cattle gate on it. Cars can drive back and forth between Bob's and Tom's property, but Tom's cattle stay on his property. Your skin is a boundary that separates you from the world even though substances cross that border constantly.

Hierarchy is how these various boundaries are arranged. A whole is made up of parts, which themselves are made up of more parts. Complex systems are often themselves made up of different complex systems. Many cells make up a tissue; many tissues, an organ; many organs, a body. And many bodies? They make up a company or a family or a society. At every level, the rules and behaviors of the parts are not the same as the rules and behaviors of the next step up in the

---

74   John Holland, *Complexity: A Very Short Introduction*, (Oxford, Oxford University Press, 2014).

hierarchy. The simple rules that govern an individual bee, when repeated across thousands of bees, create the complex, emergent behaviors of the hive. And the hive itself is a part within the larger emergent order of the ecosystem. Emergence is the result of complex parts interacting in a way to create a new whole with behaviors and rules that differ from the behaviors and rules of the parts.

A **signal** is what crosses a boundary. Signals are how various parts of a system interact with each other. This happens on many different scales. For example, a cell's boundary selectively allows certain chemicals from other cells inside, triggering a reaction within the cell which then produces new chemicals that it passes along to other cells. The pheromones of a foraging ant signals to other ants. At a much higher level, when you share a story you heard with someone else, you're passing a signal from yourself to them.

These concepts are necessarily abstract because they apply to all complex systems. In fact, the study of complex systems seeks to understand generalized principles of how *parts*, separated from each other by *boundaries* and interacting with each other through *signals*, can form a *whole* that does something different and unpredictable. How does the whole emerge as more than the sum of the parts?

ORDER EMERGES FROM CHAOS

Emergent order must emerge from something. That something is disorder, or chaos. Systems that exhibit emergent order form out of chaotic systems. The study of chaos is one of the disciplines that overlaps with the study of complex systems; you may recall from the introduction that I was inspired as a young teen by the late 1980s pop science book *Chaos: Making a New Science* by James Gleick.[75] "Chaos theory" was an early shorthand for the study of unexpectedly unpredictable phenomena. That is, in several different sciences, people were noticing that certain kinds of systems, such as seemingly simple equations, would produce unexpectedly complex, even random looking results.

One of the key findings about chaotic systems is their sensitivity to initial conditions. Chaotic systems can have wildly varying results in output even with a tiny variation in inputs. Changes to the fifth decimal place can result in entirely different patterns. Differences in inputs can create disproportionately different outputs. Such systems "can make a surprising mountain out of a molehill."[76] Colloquially this is known as the butterfly effect: the idea that a butterfly flapping its wings in Japan creates a hurricane in the Atlantic. What this often means is that scientists cannot even in theory predict chaotic systems—like the weather, for example—because their measurements of the real world are necessarily approximate. The tiny fractions by which their measurements are off from the real values make the models quickly diverge from reality.

Emergent order might sound like the opposite of a chaotic system, but in fact the two concepts are related. Chaos is necessary to the emergent order. In other words, disorder facilitates emergent order by increasing the dynamism of the

75 James Gleick, *Chaos: Making a New Science* (New York: Penguin Publishing Group, 1988).

76 John Holland, *Complexity: A Very Short Introduction*, (Oxford, Oxford University Press, 2014), 509.

system. Emergent order tends to happen right at the edge of chaos. Eliminating disorder reduces the possibility of emergent order.

For example, consider the whirlpool that forms when you pull the plug in your bathtub. That structure, a self-sustaining pattern, is only possible due to the freedom of the water molecules to jostle, interact, and flow. If the tub water were frozen, it would be more orderly and less chaotic—but a whirlpool cannot form in ice.

ATTRACTORS

Researchers who study dynamic systems talk about "attractors."[77] Attractors are positions in a system that, no matter the starting position of the system, the system tends to move toward. Think of a swing on a swing set, for example. For nearly any position I place the swing in, it will eventually return to the point closest to straight down. If I push it a little, it will swing back and forth until it stops. If I push it with a lot of force, the swing will oscillate back and forth but eventually arrive at that same spot. That spot, straight down from the swing set, is the attractor for the system. It attracts the system to that specific state.

In my swing set example—a simple system—the attractor is a single point. But complex systems often have multiple, different attractors. Which one the system is drawn to depends on the initial set up of the system. Think of a hole on a mini golf course where there is a sloping hill in the middle and

---

77 Melanie Mitchell, *Complexity: A Guided Tour*, (Oxford University Press, 2009), 30.

two different valleys that funnel the ball into different holes. Those two different holes are separate attractors. The ball's path depends on which side of the hill the initial hit sends the ball. A very small difference in the ball's original path—a fraction of an inch to the left or right—can create a very different end result. (This is another example of the sensitivity to initial conditions discussed above.)

In more complex systems, an attractor could be an entire cycle of points that the system passes through in sequence. Think again of a whirlpool. If you pull the plug in your full bathtub, a whirlpool may form, even with any number of different wave patterns in the tub. The whirlpool doesn't stay exactly the same, but it maintains a similar shape. If you stick your hand into the whirlpool, you might disrupt it, but then it will often reform. The whirlpool is an attractor.

There are also attractors where the system never quite repeats but creates a discernable mathematical pattern. These so-called strange attractors can often be quite beautiful when represented in graphical form.

The examples I have given are from physics, but attractors appear in models of many kinds of dynamic systems. In biology, attractors appear in the patterns of animal populations over time and in variations in heart rate. In finance, stock market prices exhibit characteristics of a strange attractor.

Attractors are not the same as emergent order, but they can be related. Feedback loops among many different individually acting agents can create results that look chaotic until some sort of threshold is crossed. The system can then enter a patterned output, an attractor. As one researcher described it, "the system seems to 'flip a switch' and become resilient to future disruptions—the same disruptions that drove them to criticality in the first place."[78] Thus, attractors are a way of describing the possible outcomes, or orders, of an emergent process.

For example, imagine a deer wandering across a field to a watering hole. At some point, after enough deer have followed the same path across the field, their repeated travel wears a path in the vegetation. The more vegetation is brushed aside, the more attractive that path becomes to other deer traveling in that direction, meaning the vegetation is brushed back even more frequently. This feedback loop develops a path and quickly becomes the primary way deer traverse the field. The same thing happens on college quads, such that many universities do not lay sidewalks until after frequent student pathways emerge.[79]

The concept of an attractor will be handy as a metaphor when I talk about personal habits in Chapter Nine.

AUTONOMY, CONNECTIVITY, AND FEEDBACK

Systems that exhibit emergent order are composed of many smaller components. These components have autonomy: they are not centrally controlled but act based on their own set of rules applied to the input from their environment and from the other components. Often what these individual

---

78 Kimberley Mok, "Identifying Emergent Behaviors of Complex Systems - In Nature and Computers," *The New Stack*, April 4, 2017.

79 Steve Staeger, "'Desired paths' may be the key to sidewalks at some universities," *9News*, May 24, 2018.

components can accomplish alone is surprisingly limited. The smarts come from sheer numbers. A single army ant will wander aimlessly and die quickly. One hundred army ants will demonstrate some emergent order: they will "walk around and around in never decreasing circles until they die of exhaustion."[80] "Yet put half a million together and the group as a whole becomes what some have called a 'superorganism' with 'collective intelligence.'"[81]

Complex emergent behavior can only emerge where these simple components are highly connected. One way components can be interconnected is by providing feedback to each other. Feedback is when the outputs of a system are routed back as an input to that system. If you've ever been at a public event where someone put their microphone (input) too close to their speaker (output), you know that feedback can create unpleasant effects. But feedback is critical to emergent order. As individual elements within a complex system act, they receive feedback from the world as well as other individual elements. The system evolves as individuals adjust to feedback.

There are two kinds of feedback: negative and positive. Negative feedback occurs when the change in output produces a response that reverses that change in output. When rising temperature causes a thermostat to turn off the heater, that is negative feedback. Positive feedback occurs when a change in a process's output produces a response that encourages

---

80   Melanie Mitchell, *Complexity: A Guided Tour*, (Oxford University Press, 2009), 3.

81   Ibid. 3.

further change. Audio feedback at a concert is an example of positive feedback; so is compound interest.[82]

Feedback can occur in a centralized manner; we're all familiar with feedback from our boss. But in emergent systems, feedback is decentralized. Ants don't receive commands from the queen about where to go get food; they sense pheromones from other ants on the ground. Note that in an emergent system feedback often does not contain a "plan" of any kind. The ant pheromone doesn't convey, "good job, you're walking toward the food." It just says, "Keep walking." That is why ants might circle on the same trail until they die.

I noted earlier that the price system is a classic example of emergent order. It is also a good example of feedback. Prices convey feedback to individuals. If Andy's pie shop prices are too high, customers will decide they have better ways to spend their money, cutting into Andy's profits. If Andy's prices are too low, he won't be able to afford the various inputs—ingredients, labor, rent. The prices customers are willing to pay combined with the costs of inputs will determine whether the pie shop can make a profit. If customers are not willing to pay sufficiently high prices to enable Andy to make a profit, this feedback collectively indicates that people value other uses of pie inputs (including Andy's time) more highly than they value pie. This incentivizes Andy to be more efficient in the production of his pies or may encourage him to take up a different effort altogether. If Andy can make a profit, he still has an incentive to lower costs to increase that

---

82   Robert Ulanowicz, *A Third Window: Natural Life beyond Newton and Darwin*, (Templeton Press, 2009), 64.

profit. Such feedback aligns the interests of producers and consumers across the economy with becoming more efficient in the use of scarce materials.

Biology has similar feedback loops. Our own body is full of them. Insulin responses to the consumption of sugar are one example: as blood sugar rises, the pancreas secretes insulin, which causes fat-storing cells in the body to take up more glucose, lowering the blood sugar and slowing the release of insulin. A similar but mirrored process happens when blood sugar drops below normal levels: the pancreas releases glucagon, which causes the liver to release stored glucose into the blood. Both of these processes are examples of *negative* feedback. Blood clotting is an example of positive feedback. An injured blood vessel releases chemicals that attract blood platelets, which cling to the site of the injury and release chemicals that attract more platelets. The more platelets that join the clot, the more platelets are attracted. This positive feedback accelerates clotting until the bleeding stops.

On the ecosystem level, there are many examples of both positive and negative feedback. Animal populations exhibit a positive feedback loop: the more wolves that are born, the more wolves there are to give birth. But this positive feedback loop operates within a larger negative feedback loop, where resource constraints limit the number of wolves that can survive. And of course, these wolves serve as a feedback mechanism to other species, whether it be the moose population they prey upon or the parasites that prey upon them.

Negative feedback loops are often paired (like the pancreas insulin/glucagon process) so that the result is *homeostasis*, a constant pressure to return to a "normal" state. Such feedback loops create attractors. Looking back at an earlier example, one could characterize gravity and friction as negative feedback on the position of a playground swing that returns it to the normal, resting state.

SOMETIMES EMERGENT ORDER GOES WRONG

You're on a beach. The sun is out, the breeze is salt-filled and refreshing, and the waves are sloshing their way to the shore. There's only one problem: the beach is covered in litter. You can see candy wrappers, beer cans, some plastic bags, newspapers, and a lot of other trash you cannot identify. It would be a beautiful day on a beautiful beach, but this garbage is ruining the scenery. You'd really prefer it be cleaner. In fact, you've talked to everyone who goes to that beach, and they, too, would all genuinely prefer it be cleaner. If everyone wants a cleaner beach, why does it look like a junkyard?

The answer is emergent order. Nobel Prize winning economist James M. Buchanan used this beach example in his 1976 essay *Law and the Invisible Hand* to explain that not all emergent orders are desirable.[83] He explained that cleaning up a small amount of personal trash might improve the overall cleanliness of a beach so little that people might think it reasonable to leave their trash behind. This can be true even when every single visitor would prefer a clean beach to a dirty beach. Any one visitor's trash makes little difference, but in the aggregate, the beach looks terrible. The littered

83 James M. Buchanan, "Law and the Invisible Hand," *reprinted in* The Collected Works of James M. Buchanan vol. 17 (Liberty Fund, Inc., Indianapolis, 2001), 96.

beach "order" that no one designed (indeed, no one desired) nonetheless emerges. As Buchanan says, "The forces of social evolution alone contain within their workings no guarantee that socially efficient results will emerge over time."[84]

Because emergent order can produce undesirable results, Buchanan argues that we shouldn't passively accept any and all results of collective, emergent processes. Buchanan is responding to another Nobel Prize winning economist, F.A. Hayek, for what Buchanan saw as a too simplistic view that the results of emergent order are always inherently efficient and cannot be improved upon. He disputes Hayek's conclusion that "freedom means that in some measure we entrust our fate to forces which we do not control."[85] Instead, Buchanan argues that we "must look on all institutions as improvable" and that mankind "must adopt the attitude that he can control his fate."[86]

Buchanan's narrow point that emergent order doesn't guarantee desirable outcomes is undoubtedly correct. As we've discussed, nature is packed with emergent order, and yet we as humans constantly seek to manipulate nature to meet our needs and desires. In society as well, we as individuals do not and should not just sit back and let things happen; the "order" that emerges might be unpleasant or even morally repugnant. Emergence isn't an excuse for inaction—indeed, emergent order depends on action. There can be no emergent order in a system without the action of the individuals that make up the system.

---

84 Ibid. 102.
85 Ibid. 109 n.15.
86 Ibid. 108.

Ultimately, then, emergent order is a natural phenomenon that is neither good nor bad but amoral, like gravity. We might coast along with it, like a river flowing downhill. We might fight against it, like a ship powering its way upstream. And we might harness it for other uses, like a hydroelectric dam. It is how we choose to engage with emergent order that carries moral significance. But in any case, to act without considering the effects of emergent order is akin to acting without considering the effects of gravity. That would be unwise. Much of the rest of this book is about how we should act given the existence of emergent order of all kinds.

CONCLUSION

I started this chapter by describing the examples of emergent order outside my window. That window wasn't special. Look out practically any window and you will see emergent order. Yet even though we are surrounded by examples of emergent order—indeed, we ourselves are examples—the concepts involved are complex and sometimes counterintuitive. They are, however, a critical foundation for the discussions in the rest of the book. I will frequently refer to the concepts laid out here as we explore what emergent order means for us as leaders and individuals in a complex world.

If this is all somewhat unclear, that is undoubtedly my failure to clearly capture the core of these concepts. But I hope that as we travel into the history and then the applications of these ideas, a clearer understanding will emerge.

CHAPTER 4

How Emergent Order Emerged

———

"People hate nuance," economist Russ Roberts told me one sunny DC afternoon over Zoom. Roberts is the President of Shalem College in Jerusalem, a fellow at the Hoover Institution at Stanford University, and host of the most popular economics podcast in the world, *EconTalk*. He is also one of the few academic economists who is working hard to spread the ideas of emergent order to a general audience. He has spent a large portion of his professional career breaking through people's distaste for nuance to share with them the highly nuanced concept of emergent order.

In particular, people hate nuance over who is in control. Modernity is in many ways premised on the belief that humans can control the world around them. Roberts quoted me a stanza from *Invictus* by W. E. Henley:

> *"It matters not how strait the gate*
> *How charged with punishments the scroll.*

I am the master of my fate:
I am the captain of my soul."[87]

"I loved that when I was twelve or fourteen. That was the greatest part of one of my favorite poems," Roberts told me. "Now I think it's stupid. I am not the master of my fate."

The ancients certainly didn't think they were masters of their fate. In Greek mythology, different gods drove the seasons and the weather, birth and death; the three Fates spun, measured, and cut the very thread of human life. Human destiny was at the whim of the gods. As Homer wrote in the *Iliad*:

"Like leaves on trees the race of man is found,
Now green in youth, now withering on the ground;
Another race the following spring supplies;
They fall successive, and successive rise."[88]

Do we control our fate or are our lives leaves scattered by the wind?

Roberts rejected Henley's *Invictus* but also told me that he doesn't believe he is "just a leaf that's blown here and there by forces I can't control. There is an in-between." For millennia, humanity has been exploring that space between fatalism and control, destiny and autonomy, connection and independence in literature, religion, and philosophy.

---

87 William Ernest Henley, "Invictus," Poetry Foundation, accessed March 31, 2021.

88 Homer, *The Iliad*, trans. Alexander Pope (Project Gutenberg, 2002).

The study of emergent order continues that exploration but is relatively young. One can see some similar themes in Eastern philosophy and in early Greek philosophy like stoicism. But emergent order as a generally recognized characteristic of natural and social phenomena is less than a century old. Before it was recognized as a general phenomenon, examples of emergent order were identified in two fields: economics and biology. Nobel Prize-winning economist James Buchanan called the concept that order in markets can come about without a designing mind "the great intellectual discovery of the eighteenth century."[89] Around the same time, Darwin transformed the field of biology when he described how order emerges in nature through the evolution of species.

Let's deepen our understanding of the nuanced idea of emergent order by tracing how emergent order emerged in these two fields.

EMERGENT ORDER IN ECONOMICS

The study of economics began with one man's attempt to answer an important question: why are some countries wealthy while others are poor? Emergent order was a key part of the answer, although that term wasn't used. Emergent order has remained a key theme in economics, although some scholars emphasize it more than others.

---

89 James Buchanan, *The Collected Works of James Buchanan Vol. 17: Moral Science and Moral Order* (Indianapolis, IN: Liberty Fund, 2001), 96.

ADAM SMITH AND THE SCOTTISH ENLIGHTENMENT

Why are some countries wealthy? The man asking this question was Adam Smith, the "Father of Economics." Smith was born in Scotland in the early eighteenth century. He studied philosophy, physics, and logic at Glasgow and Oxford Universities and later became a professor of logic and philosophy at Glasgow University. In 1776 he published the first volume of his well-known work, *An Inquiry into the Nature and Causes of the Wealth of Nations.*[90]

Wealth of Nations is a masterwork. One of Smith's many insights was that nations primarily become wealthy through specialization of labor. That is, people can create more wealth more efficiently when individuals (and regions) specialize in what they are best at, comparatively speaking, and then exchange their outputs with other people to satisfy other needs.

As important as this observation, however, was his explanation that specialization *emerges without design.* Instead, the desire of humans to barter and exchange pushes workers toward specialization. Where exchange is allowed and facilitated, workers become more and more specialized over time and a nation grows correspondingly wealthier because people find they can get more by exchanging specialized services.

Smith's explanation is an emergent one. Individuals acting on straightforward incentives generate a complex phenomenon—one that benefits others as well as themselves. Smith's

---

90 Adam Smith, *An Inquiry Into the Nature and Causes of the Wealth of Nations*, ed. Edwin Cannan, (London: Methuen, 1904), accessed at Online Liberty Library.

work in *Wealth of Nations* and another book, *The Theory of Moral Sentiments,* seeks to identify how the organized patterns that we see in our lives are the result of the actions of individuals but not the result of their designs.[91] Economists since Smith have sought to understand and describe the patterns that emerge from billions of individuals acting on their own knowledge and preferences.

Smith demonstrated a deep intuition for the emergent nature of human interactions, but he didn't specifically identify emergent order as a phenomenon—at least not intentionally. Perhaps Smith's most famous idea was to describe the market as containing an "invisible hand" that guides and shapes market outcomes. Smith said:

> *"It is not from the benevolence of the butcher, the brewer, or the baker, that we can expect our dinner, but from their regard to their own interest.... By directing that industry in such a manner as its produce may be of greatest value, [each] intends only his own gain, and he is in this, as in many other cases, led by an invisible hand to promote an end which was no part of his intention."*[92]

Russ Roberts, who is a scholar of Smith's work, has noted that *"invisible hand* is a nice way to describe something that looks designed but that in fact emerges from an unnoticed, unseen, and complex web of innumerable human

---

91 Adam Smith, *The Theory of Moral Sentiments*, (Neeland Media, 2018).

92 Adam Smith, *An Inquiry Into the Nature and Causes of the Wealth of Nations*, ed. Edwin Cannan, (London: Methuen, 1904), accessed at Online Liberty Library.

interactions."[93] Indeed, the invisible hand concept captures the idea that a simple local rule for merchants ("pursue self-interest") results in an emergent order of prosperity for others. That's why it's "too bad," Roberts notes, that Smith meant something more straightforward: "he simply meant self-interested actions that turn out to benefit others."[94]

But while Smith's conception of emergence was more implied than expressed, there was clearly something stirring throughout the Scottish Enlightenment. A friend of Smith's, the philosopher and founder of the study of sociology, Adam Ferguson, described in a 1782 passage one very important type of emergent order:

> *Every step and every movement of the multitude, even in what are termed enlightened ages, are made with equal blindness to the future; and nations stumble upon **establishments, which are indeed the result of human action, but not the execution of any human design.***[95]

Ferguson is describing patterns and institutions that are created by collective human effort and choices but which no one designed or controls. Think back to the earlier example of "the wave" at a baseball game. Like so much of our day-to-day life, that pattern is the result of human action but not of human design.

---

93 Russ Roberts, *How Adam Smith Can Change Your Life*, (Portfolio, 2015), 178.
94 Ibid.
95 "Adam Ferguson observed that...," Online Library of Liberty, accessed February 11, 2021.

Adam Smith is mostly known for his impact on economics, but the ideas of emergence that he and his Scottish brethren developed sowed the seeds for a much broader exploration of the emergent nature of human society and the institutions that it develops. As economist and professor Steven Horwitz explains it:

> "The liberalism rooted in the Scottish Enlightenment ... recognizes human fallibility and the subjective, tacit, and context-specific nature of much of our knowledge. It further recognizes the inherently social nature of human beings: in order to survive, we must cooperate with others. However, adherents of the spontaneous-order tradition argue that such cooperation need not and to a high degree cannot be intentional, planned cooperation. They emphasize how much of our social world has emerged as unintended consequences of human action."[96]

This is a vision of society as an emergent order of cooperation creating a beneficial whole that is greater than the sum of its imperfect human participants. It is the opposite of the common stereotype that economists assume humans are perfectly rational, perfectly informed market participants.

While "the market is the foremost example" of emergent phenomena in the human social world, the ideas from Smith and his Scottish allies influenced history, philosophy, linguistics, psychology, and especially political philosophy, ultimately

---

96 Steven Horowitz, "From Smith to Menger to Hayek: Liberalism in the Spontaneous-Order Tradition," *Independent Institute*, 6 no. 1, (2001): 95.

shaping the Enlightenment and the liberal institutions that developed.[97]

F. A. HAYEK

Those seeds, planted by the eighteenth-century Scottish intellectuals, found full economic expression in a twentieth-century Austrian. Friedrich August von Hayek was born in Vienna in 1899, the oldest of three brothers in a scholarly and well-established family during an era of great change. He would fight against the intellectual tide of his profession and world for most of his life, only to see late success and revival. Today, he is considered in the very top tier of economists of the twentieth century. His ideas continue to resonate across many fields of academia and throughout public policy debates. In particular, Hayek's idea of spontaneous order and his description of what is now known as the knowledge problem remain key to understanding how complex systems, from the human brain to society, can outperform top-down designed systems.

One quick note on terminology: Hayek used the term "spontaneous order" to discuss what I call emergent order. Many economists follow his example. However, non-economists tend to talk about emergence or emergent order. I prefer the term "emergent order" as it sounds less happenchance, accidental, or sudden. But, at least as I use them, the two terms are synonymous.

Hayek spent most of his life fighting against the centralization of power and for emergent order. But he didn't find that calling immediately. As a very young officer in World War

---

97 Ibid.

I, he saw the disaster and aftermath of war and entered the University of Vienna determined to make the world a better place. Initially, he was attracted to the growing socialist movement. That movement promised to replace the chaos of the post-WWI world with well-designed government solutions to meet every need of society. To an intelligent young man with an academic inclination, the opportunity to help design a new society must have been attractive.

Hayek entered university as a law student but became more interested in helping the world through psychology and economics. The University of Vienna was one of the top three universities in the world for economics, and Hayek took advantage of that expertise. He was earning his second doctorate at the university when one of its leading economists, Ludwig von Mises, published his book *Socialism*, a critique of socialist attempts to replace markets with centralized methods of distributing goods and services. This book changed Hayek's life. As he described it, "To none of us young men who read the book when it appeared, the world was ever the same again."[98]

Mises pointed to a fundamental flaw in the socialist plan to eliminate private property: a lack of prices. Prices convey essential information about what people need and desire and how well the current allocation of resources matches those needs. Without people generating prices by exchanging their goods for currency in a marketplace, planners "would be groping in the dark" when choosing what to produce and how.[99]

---

98 "Biography of F. A. Hayek (1899 - 1992)," Mises Institute, accessed February 24, 2021.

99 Steven Horowitz, "From Smith to Menger to Hayek: Liberalism in the Spontaneous-Order Tradition," *Independent Review* (2001): 93.

Mises saw that the market was an emergent process where others saw disorder and inefficiency. "Whereas socialists had long seen the market as irrational and anarchic," Horowitz continues, Mises showed that "the seeming anarchy of production gave rise to a rational economic order when actors could make use of market prices to guide their decisions."[100] Individual decisions in the marketplace generate information that prices convey to others, leading to an orderly allocation of resources without anyone in control.

Hayek was so taken with Mises's work that he joined Mises and others in what is known as the "Austrian school of economics"—a name drawn from the origins of this school of thought more than its current geographic location, as most of the scholars fled Austria during the buildup to World War II.

Throughout his life, Hayek generalized and extended the emergent order principle found in Mises's argument. He was particularly fond of paraphrasing Ferguson when talking about phenomena that are "the result of human action but not human design."[101] Hayek knew this concept was counterintuitive for the uninitiated. "To the naïve mind that can conceive of order only as the product of deliberate arrangement," he said, "it may seem absurd that in complex conditions, order, and adaptation to the unknown, can be achieved more effectively by decentralizing decisions, and that a division of authority will actually extend the

---

100 Ibid. 94.
101 Fredrich Hayek, "The Results of Human Action but not of Human Design." in *Studies in Philosophy, Politics and Economics* (New York, Simon and Schuster): 96–105.

possibility of overall order."[102] In other words, for those who mistakenly think that order requires a designer, it makes little sense to advocate decentralizing decision making as a way to increase order.

Hayek worked to persuade those uninitiated. He consistently emphasized the limits of what we can predict and plan when dealing with emergent phenomena like markets. "The curious task of economics," he wrote, "is to demonstrate to men how little they really know about what they imagine they can design."[103] Hayek viewed the overall economy as an ecosystem, a garden, where the task of policymakers was, by encouraging functioning institutions such as rule of law and private property, to patiently nourish the right type of environment for the emergent order of markets to flourish. When faced with economy-wide problems, Hayek's work demonstrates how poor government policy contributed to sharp booms of growth and thus to subsequent busts of de-growth. His prescriptions required long term vision and restraint by policymakers, not quick-fix methods.

Hayek's approach offered politicians facing an economic crisis with little to do except general reform to prevent the next crisis. But politicians want to deal with the current problem; they want a tool that offers them something they can do, something they can point to when running for reelection and say, "See, I acted. I did that!"

---

102 Friedrich Hayek, *The Fatal Conceit* (Chicago, University of Chicago Press, 1988), 76 - 77.
103 Ibid. 76.

Other economists offered approaches that promised to deliver what politicians wanted. Whereas Hayek described the economy as a garden, John Maynard Keynes's *The General Theory of Employment, Interest and Money*, published in 1936, conceived of the economy more like an engine that could be revved up or down by different government policies.[104] This gave politicians a metaphorical throttle to press during a crisis.

The Great Depression created an enormous desire for such economic tools to address high unemployment and brought Keynes and his approach to great prominence. The resulting Keynesian Revolution dramatically changed the study of economics as well as the purposes to which it was put.[105] Rather than study how order emerged in markets without central design, economists sought to provide the tools policy makers needed to shape markets.

During the ascendance of Keynesian economics, the ideas of emergent order remained a thread within the economics profession—what economist Peter Boettke calls "mainline economics"—but it was largely ignored in the economic mainstream. Hayek himself continued to be influential, but increasingly his influence was outside of the economic world and more in other social sciences. He wrote several books on a wide range of topics, including politics, philosophy, law and economics, and even on theoretical psychology. It was

---

104 John Maynard Keynes, *General Theory of Employment, Interest and Money* (Palgrave Macmillan, 1936).

105 Lawrence H. White, *The Clash of Economic Ideas* (Cambridge University Press, 2012), 126-127.

also during this time that Hayek penned the powerful and influential essay, "The Use of Knowledge in Society."[106]

His quiet, diligent curiosity paid off in a surprising way. In 1974, Hayek was awarded the prestigious Nobel Memorial Prize in Economic Sciences.[107] There is some debate about why the committee picked him. Some say it was to provide ideological balance to the leftist economist the committee had picked to share the prize with Hayek. Hayek himself was reportedly surprised by the award.[108]

Regardless of the reason, Hayek seized the opportunity to highlight his view of the current state of economic theory and practice. His acceptance speech was pointedly titled "The Pretence of Knowledge."[109] Delivered to an audience of distinguished economists, it was a sharp critique of the direction of the economics profession, which "had made a mess of things" because they ignore the inevitable consequences of emergent order. He said economists had tried to turn the study of humans and society into a science of prediction, like physics. Hayek argued that this was both a futile and dangerous approach. It was futile because human society, unlike the inanimate matter that physicists study, contains irreducible complexity with facts that cannot be gathered and summarized to make precise predictions.

---

106 Friedrich Hayek, "The Use of Knowledge in Society," *American Economic Review*, 35 no. 4, (1945).

107 "Friedrich August von Hayek," The Nobel Prize, accessed February 24, 2021.

108 Linda Yueh, "Friedrich Hayek's devotion to the free market," *Linda Yueh.com*, 2018.

109 Friedrich von Hayek, "The Pretence of Knowledge" (Speech, Nobel Memorial Lecture, December 11, 1974).

And this "scientistic" approach to economics was dangerous because it led economists to offer centralized solutions that actually slowed or stopped the many interactions in society that would have produced emergent solutions to complex problems. Hayek argued that if economists truly wished to improve society, they must be humble and realize the bounds of what is possible with social science. Overconfidence in the use of science to control society will make a man a tyrant, Hayek warned, and economists should worry about how their theories could be used destructively. Rather than attempting to shape society directly like a sculptor shapes a statue, Hayek encouraged his audience to instead seek to understand and to create the right environment for progress, like a gardener in a garden.[110]

Hayek's criticism of his fellow economists was received with cool and polite applause, but the outside world was hungry for those ideas. While Hayek was critical of the Nobel Prize and skeptical of his profession, receiving the reward reinvigorated his career and launched his ideas and the ideas of the Austrian school of economics to new prominence. Hayek's work was touted by the most powerful and popular politicians of that era, Margaret Thatcher and Ronald Reagan, as major influences on their thinking and policies—although Hayek himself wrote an entire essay, "Why I Am Not a Conservative."[111]

Indeed, many of the insights of the Austrian school are being rediscovered by a growing body of economics that

---

110 *See generally*, Neil Chilson, "A Simplified 'Pretence of Knowledge," *Neil Chilson* (blog), April 4, 2016.

111 Friedrich Hayek, "Why I am not a Conservative," (1960).

emphasizes the imperfect decision-making of individuals. The field behavioral economics has developed in reaction to mainstream neoclassical economics that dominated the latter half of the twentieth century. Neoclassical economists emphasize mathematical models based on assumptions about individuals as purely rational decision-makers with perfect knowledge who seek to maximize utility. Behavioral economists push back on that assumption, seeking to blend economics and psychology and using empirical experiments to show that certain neoclassical premises are, at best, oversimplifications and, at worst, are entirely wrong.

Economists in the emergent order tradition would find many of the criticisms from behavioral economists both obvious and somewhat irrelevant. Functional markets do not require objectively rational, fully informed decision-makers any more than an operational anthill requires omniscient worker ants. As Professor Horwitz explains:

> "[U]nlike neoclassical economics and the traditions of liberalism that make use of it, liberalism in the spontaneous-order tradition does not rest on any belief about the rationality of human actors. In fact, the case for this kind of liberalism is predicated on our ignorance. Because so much of our knowledge is tentative, fragmented, and tacit, we require the use of spontaneously evolved social institutions to generate social order. Spontaneous-ordering processes are communication procedures that enable us to overcome our very narrow and partial views of the world and to make use of the differently partial and narrow knowledge that others possess. In this tradition, it is not the individual actors

that are best described as 'rational,' but the processes in which they operate."[112]

In other words, markets (and other liberal institutions) are an emergent phenomenon that we rely upon to produce rational results despite the inadequacies of any one market participant.

To be fair, it's not as if mainstream economists are fully ignorant of emergent order. Most would agree with the basic premise, identified by Smith, that markets enable individuals to act on individual knowledge and coordinate behavior in highly sophisticated ways without anyone being in charge. But in some ways their familiarity with one expression of emergent order, markets, constrains their ability to realize the wide applicability of the concept. Professor Russ Roberts, during the Zoom call I opened the chapter with, told me the story of giving a seminar on emergent order to a room full of serious PhD economists and just watching their brains switch off. "They were so unimpressed," he told me. "They were like, 'Oh, this is basic, we know all about that.' But they didn't."

Emergent order is a foundational concept of economics. The extent to which many modern economists are not expressly aware of it is a shame because understanding it would help temper their expectations about shaping and designing interventions. Still, economists are probably more attuned to emergent order than any other major academic field— except biologists!

---

112 Steven Horwitz, "From Smith to Menger to Hayek: Liberalism in the Spontaneous Order Tradition", *Independent Review* 6 no. 1, (2001): 91-92.

EMERGENT ORDER AND EVOLUTIONARY BIOLOGY

In contrast to modern economists, many of whom aren't expressly aware of the emergent nature of the phenomena they study, you'd be hard-pressed to find a biologist ignorant or dismissive of the emergent phenomena at the center of their field: evolution. As an explanation for why and how lifeforms change over time, evolution was perhaps the most controversial idea in the history of science—and one of the most profound.

The discovery of evolution is most closely and famously associated with Charles Darwin. Darwin, in the mid-1800s, proposed that species evolve over time through natural selection. In competing for resources, organisms with traits better adapted to the environment will reproduce more often and therefore pass on those traits to their offspring. Offspring will also have other random variations in traits. Over long periods of time, these gradual variations and selection pressures from the environment can reshape species.

Many people are familiar with the story about Darwin's voyage on the HMS *Beagle*. Darwin, a late bloomer whose father worried that he would amount to nothing, set sail at the age of twenty-two as a naturalist and a dining companion to the ship's captain. He sailed with the *Beagle* for almost five years around South America and islands in the Pacific. Darwin kept very detailed notes about the journey, including the different varieties of animals and plants he encountered. He was particularly intrigued by the variation in otherwise similar wildlife depending on the conditions around the animals.[113]

---

113 "Charles Darwin: A Short Biography," Discovery Institute, accessed February 24, 2021.

The most famous example Darwin offers is the variation in the beaks of otherwise similar finches on the various Galapagos islands. Each different type of finch beak was well-adapted to the food sources on that specific island—thick beaks to crack nuts or seeds and long, thin beaks for insects or other food sources. Darwin theorized that all the finches came from a common ancestor and that natural selection on each island shaped the beaks of the finches over time.

Melanie Mitchell, in her excellent book *Complexity: A Guided Tour*, details four key ideas in Darwin's theory, which (slightly paraphrased) are:

- All species descended from a common ancestor.
- Natural selection occurs when births exceed the resources available to support individuals, forcing them to compete.
- Organisms inherit traits from their ancestors, with variation. Variations that increase the likelihood that the organism survives become more common in subsequent generations of organisms.
- Evolutionary change is gradual but constant, with small favorable changes accumulating over time to form big differences.

As Mitchell summarizes, "According to this view, the result of evolution by natural selection is the appearance of 'design' but with no designer."[114] In other words, complex biological organisms are a result of emergent order.

---

114 Melanie Mitchell, *Complexity: A Guided Tour* (Oxford University Press, 2009), 78-79.

But the study of evolution didn't stop with these four ideas. Darwin didn't know how traits were passed on from parent to child. The discovery of genetics and DNA (the complex chemical chains in cells that encode genes) explained this, but also added a lot of complexity. The early assumption was that individual sequences of DNA control a single physical trait, such as blue eyes, on a one-to-one basis. Subsequent research has demonstrated that genes are the expression of multiple strands of DNA, and that DNA sequences are networks, with various sequences influencing and affecting the expression of other sequences.[115] That is, complex feedback loops exist within the genetic sequences themselves.

This research has brought into question some of Darwin's key tenets. Some biologists argue that evolutionary change need not be gradual. Genetic mechanisms contain feedback loops that can produce periods of relatively rapid change, or *punctuated equilibria*, these researchers contend. Natural selection may operate at the species level, others argue. Some challenge the notion that natural selection is the primary force in evolution: Stephen Jay Gould, for example, argues that many traits are not "adaptions" that increase survival as much as they are the result of historical accidents or pure biological constraints.[116] Others, such as theoretical biologist Stuart Kauffman, are even more radical. He has argued that the complexity of the genetic feedback loops are themselves self-organizing. "[L]ife has an innate tendency to become

115 Ibid. 273-77.
116 Ibid.

more complex" independent of natural selection, as Dr. Mitchell summarizes this view.[117]

We still do not know enough about the mechanics of DNA and genes to settle many of these questions, and the debates continue. These debates generally take place outside the public eye in part because some evolutionary biologists worry that admitting that there is much more to learn about evolution somehow concedes ground to "intelligent design" advocates who criticize evolutionary theory, primarily on religious grounds.[118] This chilling effect has a long history: Darwin didn't publish *On the Origin of Species* until 1859, more than twenty-three years after his voyage on the *Beagle*, in part out of concerns about the religious implications of his work.[119]

And yes, even more than a hundred years later, many see the theory of evolution as a threat to their religious beliefs. I myself worry what some of my family members will think about this part of this book. But I personally do not see an inherent conflict between our biology as an emergent system and belief in an omnipotent and omniscient God. It no more worries me that our biology is emergent than it does that our markets or cities are emergent. In fact, the more I have learned about the complexity of DNA and its expression in the amazing variety of life across the earth, the more in awe I am of how little we know, and how beautiful even that little bit is. It also makes me humble about dictating what others must think.

---

117 Ibid. 286.
118 Ibid. 287.
119 Ibid. at 77. *See* Charles Darwin, *On the Origin of Species by Means of Natural Selection* (John Murray, 1859).

But this is not the right place for that debate. The simple point here is that emergent order is central to evolutionary biology and has been since Darwin.

FROM ECONOMICS AND BIOLOGY TO A SCIENCE OF ITS OWN

Steven Johnson's book *Emergence* describes how the study of emergent order moved through three historical phases. In phase one researchers across a wide range of fields—economics, biology, meteorology, physics, etc.—sought to recognize and understand various complex systems without realizing there was a coherent principle joining their research. In the second phase, scholars began to make connections across various fields and realized that emergent order itself was an independent phenomenon worth studying. In the third phase, according to Johnson, where we are now, researchers have started creating artificial systems that rely on emergent order to recommend movies, recognize our voices, or populate game environments.

Adam Smith, Adam Ferguson, and Charles Darwin fall squarely in phase one. They observed and analyzed emergent order within their specific discipline but didn't seek to understand it as an independent phenomenon across disciplines. We've talked a lot about them already.

Johnson's third phase, interpreted broadly, is about how we learn to adapt to and benefit from emergent order. I see this book as part of that phase.

To be effective in phase three, however, it's worth a short detour into phase two. That phase progressed in fits and starts, partly due to its cross-disciplinary nature. For example, Hayek was primarily in phase one, but "The Use of Knowledge in Society" and other works bridge into the second phase. Like Hayek, others spotted principles of emergence and complex systems and started to connect those ideas across disciplines.

In the 1980s, these cross-disciplinary efforts found an institutional home at the Santa Fe Institute (SFI). SFI, hosted in an old convent in Santa Fe, New Mexico, started as the dream of one chemist, George Cowan, to reconcile the sciences with the humanities. He believed that chemistry and other hard sciences had much to offer to society beyond the application of science to specific problems. He wanted science to cross-pollinate with the humanities in order to pursue the study of complex systems. Despite this mixing pot goal, early on the Institute was dominated by personalities like physicists David Pines, Murray Gell-Mann, Philip Anderson, and other highly credentialed hard science scholars. Early participants in SFI events included many Nobel Prize winners.[120]

Though dominated by physicists and the like, the Institute gained its first permanent track of research due to a social science failure to foresee a financial crisis. In 1986, John Reed at Citibank agreed to fund an SFI workshop on "The Economy as an Evolving Adaptive System." Reed wanted to know why his economists at Citibank had completely missed a financial crisis in Latin America. That crisis had cost the bank sorely, and Reed wanted answers and new approaches.[121]

---

120 "History: Santa Fe Institute," Santa Fe Institute, accessed February 24, 2021.
121 Ibid.

The weeklong workshop brought together physicists and economists to tackle economic problems. It was co-led by Nobel Prize-winning physicist Phil Anderson and Nobel Prize-winning economist Kenneth Arrow. The atmosphere was charged, with physicists seeming hardly to believe how mathematically abstract the economics field was. One participant quipped, "I used to think that physicists were the most arrogant people in the world. The economists were, if anything, more arrogant." As one article reporting on the event summarized:

> *"The economists felt physical scientists could not possibly help with their problems, and the physical scientists thought economics was a mess and there was not much you could do with it."*[122]

Indeed, the two groups took very different approaches to problem-solving. Because the physical scientists had access to a lot of data, they tended toward empirical work, experimenting with different approaches and building simulations. Economists (at least at that time) had much less raw data, and, therefore relied heavily on theoretical analysis and rigorous mathematical models from baseline assumptions.

One of the baseline assumptions that particularly bothered the physicists was the then-dominant Arrow-Debreu model's assumption that economic agents (individuals) make perfectly rational predictions about the future and then act to maximize the expected outcomes.[123] To physicists, who know that

122 Robert Pool, "Strange Bedfellows," *Science*, August, 1989, 703.
123 Ibid. 702.

predicting the weather a day in advance is dicey, this "rational expectations" hypothesis seemed a shaky assumption.

Indeed, the early work of SFI's economic complexity program tackled how to replace the rational expectations hypothesis with a more realistic model. Others in the program sought answers to the more general problem of how to model complex economic systems.

Thirty-plus years after that first meeting of physicists and economists at SFI, not much progress has been made in replacing the rational expectations hypothesis with a complex systems model, and the Institute's influence on mainstream economics has been slight. Economic research has changed. Empirical methods and experiments are much more common in the economics profession, but those trends grew out of the work of other economists, not the complexity researchers at SFI. Rationality is still a widely used assumption for economic agents, even though most agree it is an oversimplification. And most models of the economy are "simplistic caricatures of the real world," according to economist and SFI external scholar Rob Axtell.[124] Modern experience makes it pretty clear that economists are not significantly better at identifying or predicting market events in the twenty-first century than they were in the twentieth.

I interviewed Axtell, who chairs the Department of Computational Social Science at George Mason University, to

---

124 Rob Axtell and J. Doyne Farmer, "Predicting the Next Recession," in *Worlds Hidden in Plain Sight: Thirty Years of Complexity Thinking at the Santa Fe Institute*, ed. David C. Krakauer (Santa Fe Institute Press, 2019), 245.

learn more about the intersection between SFI and economics. Particularly, why haven't economists absorbed or created more complex systems research? He explained that the mathematics of complex systems are very challenging to compute. His own specific field of economic study, agent-based modeling, uses millions of relatively simple computer programs to represent individual firms and households and simulates them interacting with each other over time (a good example of Johnson's third phase of the study emergence, creation). Computers have only recently become capable of efficiently simulating economy-scale numbers of these agents. So, economists and computer scientists are still learning to apply some of the ideas that originated in the early days of SFI. He also explained that academia changes slowly. Axtell is optimistic that the coming generation of economists will have the mathematical chops, inquiring spirit, and computational tools to explore the questions that the Santa Fe Institute has been asking for thirty years.

Still, the best evidence suggests that what John Reed sought from that 1986 conference is unachievable to the degree he would have liked. He wanted the ability to predict market events to control them. Because complex systems can arise from simple rules executed by smaller, independent decision-makers, the hope seemed to be that if we could discover simple rules, we could better predict the behavior of the system. Axtell's agent-based approach flips that on its head, assuming some reasonable rules for the behavior of agents but relying on the simulated interactions between the agents to generate insights. However, these insights won't be predictions of where the economy will be at some point in the future and these models wouldn't help John Reed make better trades on Wall Street. Instead, by running a simulation thousands of times, Axtell hopes to "show policy makers the range of possible future outcomes and their relative probabilities" under various policy choices.[125]

To my mind, complex system thinking in economics continues the mainline of emergent order throughout history, helping us discover new principles about the world around us while reminding us there are things we cannot predict or control.

Of course, while the Reed funding contributed to the early shape and subsequent trajectory of SFI, economics was just one of the fields the Santa Fe Institute hoped to integrate. The bigger, overarching project was to identify tools that could be applied to any domain with emergent phenomena to identify, understand, and hopefully control emergent systems. Though the Santa Fe Institute was early on dominated by hard scientists, today it is much closer to the cross-pollination of science and humanities of which George Cowan dreamed.

Perhaps it is that greater diversity in scholars as well as thirty years of struggle that has shifted SFI's research emphasis away from the control of complex systems and toward a more nuanced approach to complexity and emergent order. This shift can be seen in a 2019 collection of essays by edited by SFI President David C. Krakauer. The collection, "Worlds Hidden in Plain Sight: Thirty Years of Complexity Thinking at the Santa Fe Institute," starts with

---

125 Ibid. 247.

essays from the late 1980s and the 1990s with titles like "Can Physics Contribute to Economics?" and "Learning How to Control Complex Systems." But the final paragraph of the collection, from an essay by Krakauer, calls for engineers to embrace "a maturation in our willingness to live with relatively high levels of uncertainty in the domains of complex phenomena—and thus give up on ideas like complete 'cures,' the elimination of 'risk,' the design of perfect 'stability,' and achieving total 'security.'"[126]

Instead, as we move into Johnson's third stage of emergence—creation—Krakauer would have us replace such "ideals of a deterministic age with an understanding of the ever-evolving nature of adaptive processes."[127] In other words, we should relax our pursuit for control and instead search for methods that can move us toward outcomes that are acceptable, adaptable, and evolving, but never perfect.

CONTROLLING, OR CONTROLLED BY, COMPLEXITY?

The study of emergent order has itself emerged. It first developed within economics and biology, but it now spans fields as seemingly disparate as physics, urban planning, genetics, and political science.

Each step along the way continued the age-old debate over whether we are the masters of our fates or merely leaves blown about by forces far greater than ourselves. Can we

---

126 *Worlds Hidden in Plain Sight: Thirty Years of Complexity Thinking at the Santa Fe Institute*, ed. David C. Krakauer (Santa Fe Institute Press, 2019), 355.

127 Ibid.

control the complex systems around us? Or are we controlled by them?

As much as people might hate it, emergent order's answer is nuanced. Learning those nuances is key to effective leadership in this complex world, as we'll see in the next chapter.

CHAPTER 5

Leadership
Without Control

Is there any type of organization less emergent and more concerned with control than the military? Militaries have a predetermined and quite static hierarchy of ranks, seek to train soldiers into specific skill sets, and have a chain of command that dictates who is in command. And yet, in complex situations, and even when the stakes are enormous, true leadership requires letting go of control—even in the military.

General Stanley McChrystal realized this when, despite having the overwhelming superiority in firepower, manpower, intelligence, and resources, the Joint Special Operations Command Task Force in Iraq that he led was continually surprised by Iraqi terrorist leader Abu Musab al-Zarqawi and other Al Qaeda in Iraq forces. The Task Force couldn't keep up with al-Zarqawi's smaller, poorly trained extremist forces. McChrystal identified one cause of the Task Force's sluggishness: the need for senior command to approve every major decision. The exertion of control by the top commanders—specifically, McChrystal himself—was a tactical liability. Although being asked to approve decisions made him feel important and like a leader, he realized he was often merely rubber-stamping the better-informed recommendations of his trusted team. And that hurdle not only wasn't adding value, but it also hamstrung the soldiers in the field, preventing quick responses to changing circumstances.

McChrystal's solution, discussed at length in his book *Team of Teams: New Rules of Engagement for a Complex World*, was to become more "Hands Off," as the title of one of the chapters puts it.[128] While modern information technology gave him the ability to know much more about the individual actions of units on the ground, that transparency was no substitute for decision-making closer to the situation. Pushing all decisions up to commanders, or even to the White House, simply didn't scale.

Instead, McChrystal decentralized decision-making, ensuring his teams had a shared culture, clearly understood the overall mission, and shared information transparently. He then trusted his teams to make decisions in the fast-developing arena they found themselves. This sped up decision-making and enabled the Task Force to make real progress against Al-Qaeda in Iraq.

McChrystal's loosening control enabled emergent order in what was a too-rigidly hierarchical organization. The way he

---

128 Stanley McChrystal, *Team of Teams: New Rules of Engagement for a Complex World*, (Penguin Random House LLC, New York, 2015), 201.

transformed the Task Force is an excellent example of how to lead in a world of complexity.

CONTROL SUPPRESSES EMERGENCE

General McChrystal realized that insisting on control was preventing the bottom-up emergent order that would enable the Joint Special Operations Task Force to accomplish its mission. Kevin Kelly, co-founder and former editor of *WIRED* magazine, explains the inevitable tradeoffs between control and emergence in his wonderful book *Out of Control*. He lists five strengths of "swarm systems," what he calls emergent systems made up of many of independent units with complex interconnections (such as ant colonies, beehives, or human society).[129] Such systems are:

- *Adaptable*: Emergent systems can adjust to unanticipated circumstances, maintaining a whole even as pieces die off or change.
- *Evolvable*: Emergent systems do more than just adapt— they can change functionality over time, both at the unit and the system level.
- *Resilient*: Failure of some parts of an emergent system can increase the strength of the overall system.
- *Boundless*: Emergent systems can grow without clear limits. In fact, they have feedback loops that generate new and different kinds of order as the size of the system grows.

---

129 Kelly calls such systems "swarm systems." Kevin Kelly, *Out of Control: The New Biology of Machines, Social Systems, and the Economic World*, (Basic Books, New York, 1994), 21-22.

- *Novel*: Compared to linear hierarchical systems, emergent systems generate unexpected results because they tolerate and even thrive on variation at the individual level and because the network of interconnections among individuals can transform minor variation into disproportionately large effects.[130]

In short, these systems are better able to take advantage of new, unanticipated opportunities, absorb and adapt to failure and use it to grow stronger over time, and be endlessly creative.

These characteristics are extremely desirable. They are the exact traits that enable organizations to thrive in a complex world. But these properties come with necessary trade-offs. These five positive traits come inseparably bound with five apparent weaknesses, says Kelly.

- *Non-optimal*: Emergent systems are resilient specifically because they are redundant, often massively so, creating amazing ability to persevere under failure but usually with great inefficiency.
- *Non-controllable*: Emergent systems have no central authority; thus, such systems cannot be commanded or directed.
- *Non-predictable*: As a direct consequence of their boundless ability to be novel, we cannot anticipate how emergent systems will adapt and evolve, especially over the long term.
- *Non-understandable*: Such systems cannot be described in terms of cause and effect because the interconnected

---

130 Kevin Kelly, *Out of Control: The New Biology of Machines, Social Systems, and the Economic World*, (Basic Books, New York, 1994), 21-22.

nature of emergent systems means everything causes everything else.

- *Non-immediate*: Even if you have all the right ingredients, emergent systems don't just turn on and off—they take time to get going as the connections between the parts are generated and refined.[131]

Such weaknesses challenge leaders who engage with emergent systems. It is easier to manipulate and direct efficient, easy-to-duplicate systems that we can understand, predict, and ultimately control. We often equate power and control with leadership. We commonly think of bosses, managers, and other leaders as in control. Many companies, bosses, and managers encourage that perception. Control often seems essential to leadership itself. After all, what does it even mean to lead in a system you cannot predict, understand, or control?

THE FADING ILLUSION OF LEADERSHIP IN CONTROL

In fact, it turns out that, like General McChrystal, most great leaders would recognize a lack of control as a common situation.

Our increasingly complex world has made more obvious what has always been the case: leaders don't control as much as they (and we) think they do. It is comforting to believe one is in control and it feeds the ego, too. In reality, leaders delegate enormous amounts of the control that they nominally exercise to others. The practical exercise of power by

---

131 Kevin Kelly, *Out of Control: The New Biology of Machines, Social Systems, and the Economic World*, (Basic Books, New York, 1994), 23.

one individual relies on acquiescence by many others. In another way, because of our tribal instincts and attraction to simplified "Great Man" narratives (more about this in Chapter Ten), followers want to believe that leaders are in control. This makes it something of a self-fulfilling prophecy. When seeking to direct a large group of individuals, convincing them that leaders are in control is an effective way—perhaps the only way—to maintain that control.

But modern information technology has undermined these misapprehensions. In the past, leaders' egos were spared by a lack of information. Leaders often thought they had control because they didn't have actual information about what they nominally controlled. Hierarchy and command-and-control were the best we could do, and nobody thought much about how little control they exercised.

Ironically, the increased flow of information has created an initial grasping for control. General McChrystal noted that his increased ability to get detailed information and communications about the situations that soldiers faced created an assumption that leadership would therefore need to sign off on every decision.[132] A Civil War general had no way to plausibly micromanage units on a mission. The operations were decentralized by necessity. The rise of real-time information and communications infrastructure seemed to remove that necessity. McChrystal's insight was that, in fact, even with additional information, decentralized decision-making was still vital.

---

132 Stanley McChrystal, *Team of Teams: New Rules of Engagement for a Complex World*, (Penguin Random House LLC, New York, 2015), 201.

Increased information flow has also undermined the illusion of leaders being in control by putting individuals at all levels of leadership on more level playing field, at least in the battle of communications. Anybody can very publicly and directly criticize leaders on social media. That kind of expression can grow to be quite powerful as others online reinforce and repeat the message. It's maybe a bit of an exaggeration to say that tweets can topple governments, but decentralized online movements have certainly amplified stories that brought down people who have been powerful and "in control" for decades—just think of the #MeToo movement.

The mental decoupling of leadership from control is beginning to be recognized by leaders across business, as well. Consider these definitions of leadership collected by Jason Morgan for his book *The Future Leader*:[133]

"Leadership is helping people succeed, inspiring and uniting people behind a common purpose and then being accountable."

— PAUL POLMAN, FORMER CEO, UNILEVER

"Leadership is about helping others realize their potential and inspiring them to work with you to achieve a shared vision for the future."

— KATHY MAZZARELLA, CEO, GRAYBAR

---

133 Jacob Morgan, "15 Top CEOs Share Their Definition of 'Leadership,'" What's Yours?," *Medium*, August 13, 2020.

"Leadership is getting people to willingly go someplace they wouldn't go themselves"

— TOM WILSON, CEO, ALLSTATE

None of these definitions (or the other eleven collected by Morgan) define leaders as those with superior understanding, knowledge of the future, or control over others. Leadership as defined by the CEOs above is a trait that anyone can exhibit, including people with no special knowledge or control. I really like how Kevin Kruse, an employee engagement expert, defines leadership: "Leadership is a process of social influence, which maximizes the efforts of others, towards the achievement of a goal."[134]

This is leadership as an input to an emergent process. This is leadership without control.

THE BUSINESS BENEFITS OF LEADERSHIP WITHOUT CONTROL

The idea that innovative organizations benefit from leadership without control isn't completely novel, at least in the business world. "Nobody has really recommended command-and-control leadership for a long time," notes MIT Professor of Management Deborah Ancona and her colleagues in their 2019 *Harvard Business Review* article on "Nimble Leadership." Yet "no fully formed alternative has emerged," and many company executives struggle to cede

---

134 Kevin Kruse, "What is Leadership," *Forbes*, April 9, 2013.

control.[135] There are templates to follow, however. Certain companies have succeeded at maintaining an entrepreneurial spirit and innovation over decades and through rapidly changing business environments. Ancona and her colleagues studied Silicon Valley R&D lab PARC and the privately held materials science company W. L. Gore & Associates. They highlight two environments rich with structure and culture that enable emergent order. These characteristics include:

- Distributed leadership at all levels of the rather flat organizations
- Widely shared cultural values and simple rules (such as Gore's rule that contracts with partners must be fair to the partner)
- Lots of small bets and experiments led by anyone with an idea
- Employees who are free to move from less promising projects to more promising ones at will
- Robust, collective decision-making norms
- Funding that expands for projects gaining steam and staff
- Deep investments in mentoring and information sharing

According to the authors, these characteristics at PARC and Gore have enabled "a whole greater than the sum of its parts" that is adaptive, innovative, and nimble. Near the end of their article, they note:

> *"Academics use the word 'emergence' to describe a process whereby order at the system level arises from*

---

135   Elaine Backman and Kate Isaacs, "Nimble Leadership," *Harvard Business Review*, July - August, 2019.

individual interaction at lower levels of aggregation.
We saw that play out at PARC and Gore."[136]

Other business leaders have embraced emergence and leadership without control. I've learned a lot about leadership from Charles Koch, chairman and CEO of Koch Industries and one of the most successful businessmen in the world. (He is also the founder of Stand Together, the philanthropic community where I am the senior research fellow for technology and innovation.) Koch evolved a small, narrowly focused family firm into one of the largest privately held companies, growing it seven-thousand-fold and outperforming the S&P 500 by more than 30-to-1.[137]

Charles Koch succeeded by applying principles that he had learned from his study of the history of scientific and social progress. The framework he developed is called Market-Based Management™, and as the moniker surely reveals, it is a framework that seeks to foster beneficial emergent order.

Charles Koch tells a story of his earliest days of taking over the family business in the 1960s and what he found:

> *"Control and protectionism ruled the day. Managers*
> *thought they always knew best, believing that their*
> *ideas were naturally superior to those of the rank-and-*
> *file... For example, the president of Koch Engineering*
> *would send questionnaires weekly to his subordinates,*

---

136 Ibid.

137 Charles Koch, *Continually Transforming Koch Industries Through Virtuous Cycles of Mutual Benefit*, (Koch Industries, 2020), 3.

making them explain each expense item, no matter how small. As a result, they had much less time for productive work."[138]

The result was a company that had "neither the vision nor the willingness to work to improve" and was "on a fast track to nowhere."[139]

The solution, Charles concluded, was to enable emergent order by inspiring and empowering the employees at all levels. This approach would later become one of the seven Guiding Principles of MBM, self-actualization: "Be a lifelong learner and realize your potential, which is essential for fulfillment. As you become increasingly self-actualized you will better deal with reality, face the unknown, creatively solve problems and help others succeed."[140]

Charles Koch explained that if employees had the chance to transform themselves, "they would transform the company, and in turn help transform society."[141] He believed that his role, and the role of every leader at the company, was to foster a culture of self-actualization. Importantly, he realized, such self-actualization cannot be imposed:

> *"Virtuous cycles, whether individual or organizational, can only occur from the bottom up, as individuals*

138 Charles Koch and Brian Hooks, *Believe in People: Bottom-up Solutions for a Top-Down World*, (St. Martin's, 2020), 64.
139 Ibid.
140 Ibid. 260 – 261.
141 Ibid. 65.

*develop and apply their abilities and as organizations
do the same with their capabilities."*[142]

In other words, a leader's role is not primarily to direct the
actions of employees, but to help employees to internalize the
values of the organization. That empowers the employee to
make autonomous decisions based on their unique talents
and knowledge, thereby creating value for the organization
and its partners.

This decentralized approach has been successful at Koch
Industries because it enables emergent order. This approach
works not just in companies but in any organization where
humans seek to cooperate to accomplish a common goal.
Within any organization, leadership without control is
not only possible, but also powerful, as the sustained success at companies like PARC, Gore, and Koch Industries
demonstrates.

Indeed, Charles Koch has pioneered applying what I call
emergent leadership not just in business but also to tackle
the biggest problems we as society face. He describes this
approach in his new book, co-authored with Stand Together
chairman and CEO Brian Hooks. Titled *Believe in People:
Bottom-Up Solutions for a Top-Down World,* the book's core
thesis is that "the combined efforts of millions of people, each
using their unique knowledge and abilities, are what improve
the world."[143] Koch's vision is of a world where all people are

---

142 Charles Koch, *Continually Transforming Koch Industries Through Virtuous Cycles of Mutual Benefit,* (Koch Industries, 2020), 5.

143 Charles Koch and Brian Hooks, *Believe in People: Bottom-up Solutions
for a Top-Down World,* (St. Martin's, 2020), 3.

empowered to follow "their own best path to contributing to the lives of others."[144] The book lays out "a vision of openness, inclusion, and empowerment based on a deep belief in people," and explains how the principles that made Koch Industries so successful can likewise help "build a better society where everyone has the opportunity to succeed."[145] Such a society would be one of ubiquitous emergent leadership.

Believe in People describes a decentralized approach to improving the world. Koch has applied that approach in the Stand Together philanthropic community that he helped found, as well as in other nonprofit organizations that he leads such as the Charles Koch Institute and the Charles Koch Foundation. The cultures of these organizations are infused with Market-Based Management. The jargon can be a bit daunting—after three years, I'm still learning what some terms mean—but the terms aren't the important part. The guiding principles of principled entrepreneurship, self-actualization, transformation, and humility directly reflect a decentralized approach, making these organizations uniquely nimble and vibrant environments for emergent solutions to difficult problems.

CHOOSING EMERGENT SOLUTIONS TO EMERGENT PROBLEMS

As organizations have adopted more emergence-facilitating structures and cultures, it is worth reminding ourselves that emergence can create problems as well as solutions. In fact, in

---

144 Ibid. 4.
145 Ibid. 6.

our world of complexity, many of the biggest problems we are dealing with themselves exhibit emergent properties. Recall Buchanan's litter-filled beach from Chapter Three as just one example of an unsatisfactory status quo. Such undesirable results can be produced by emergent order, human design, or some blend of the two.

When faced with such a situation, what kind of action should leaders take? How might someone approach trying to solve Buchanan's littered beach problem? She has choices. She could lobby local government for a top-down solution, such as laws punishing littering. By raising the otherwise small cost of littering, such laws could strengthen the incentives of individuals to clean up after themselves, correcting the externality.

Another approach might be seeking to shift the social norms of the beachgoers, perhaps through awareness campaigns or cleanup events. The goal would be for people to pride themselves on the cleanliness of the beach. A community of beachgoers who don't just desire a clean beach but take pride in it would pick up not only their own trash, but also trash from others or even trash that washes up from the ocean. Imagine a community where beachgoers would be ashamed if they walked past litter without picking it up—and where they might look askance at someone who purposely littered. This social norms campaign also changes the incentives of individuals, but in a bottom-up way.

Which of these two solutions, if established, is more sustainable and adaptable? Which could help a community deal not just with litter problems but with related natural phenomena like storm debris or dune erosion? More personally, which community would you prefer to join? One where people do the bare minimum to keep a location clean out of fear of the law or one where they take pride in their part of maintaining a clean and beautiful beach? I'd prefer the one with good neighbors rather than the one with strict laws.

To be clear, because emergent order is a characteristic of society, both solutions operate within a greater framework of emergence. (Remember the discussion of hierarchy and boundaries from Chapter Three.) New laws, top-down in design, still require enforcement, which can be shaped by any number of emergent phenomena, such as discretion or bias. And laws, by punishing certain behavior, can also shape emergent norms. For example, an anti-littering law could spur additional social contempt for litterbugs—or it could suggest to people that littering is a problem they can leave to the police.

But the social, community-oriented approach uses and amplifies emergent order while the law enforcement approach resists it or perhaps indirectly shapes it. For relatively simple-to-define problems like Buchanan's littered beach, the trade-offs of a centralized approach might be relatively minor. But for areas where even defining the problem itself is difficult—problems like poverty, opportunity, and decentralized terrorism—the trade-offs between static, top-down solutions reliant on illusory control versus nimble, dynamic, and adaptive, though messy, emergent processes can be very stark indeed.

THE NEED TO GET MESSY

The processes of emergent systems don't always produce attractive results. But asserting control to address these unattractive results can backfire. In fact, sometimes good policy outcomes require a tolerance for disorder and relinquishing control, as I learned from George Mason University Professor of Economics and Philosophy Peter Boettke. Boettke, a New Jersey-born economist, spent years studying how countries emerged from communism in the late 1980s and early 1990s. He had a front row seat to these developments, spending time during that period in Moscow as an Academy of Sciences Fellow in Moscow, and then studying and lecturing throughout eastern Europe for several years after.

On one trip to Bucharest, during after-lecture drinks with students and faculty, Boettke was asked to solve a dilemma. Like many Soviet-style economies, Romania had single-purpose towns where every resident worked to produce steel. Seventy-five miles outside of Bucharest were several of these steel towns. As the communist regime in Romania had collapsed and the government had begun to institute market reforms, these steel towns maintained 100 percent unemployment.

Professor Boettke was puzzled. Surely no town could have 100 percent unemployment—at least, not for long. But if such a situation were in fact static and self-sustaining, it would be a failure of order to emerge from what everyone agreed was a mess. Digging deeper, Boettke learned that the government was paying everyone in those towns 75 percent of their previous wages in order to keep them from leaving the towns and coming to Bucharest. Furthermore, the steel factories had German investors willing to purchase the raw materials of the closed steel mills. But the government had banned that sale—again, freezing the old system in place in hopes of an orderly transition from communist planning to free markets.

To Boettke, then, the sustained 100 percent unemployment number wasn't hard to explain. The Romanian government, by seeking to maintain control over the situation, had halted a necessary, if messy and painful, process of transition, leaving entire towns mired in an awkward transitional state like a butterfly half-emerged from a cocoon. "Every emergent order starts from an emergent mess," Boettke explained to me. That messiness is necessary for order to emerge. "If you try to stop the messiness, the messiness instead gets stuck." Boettke advised that the government facilitate the transition by relaxing control, allowing the assets to be sold and people to move on to other opportunities. In other words, to get the emergent order "whirlpool" of markets, the city had to be unfrozen.

The difficult and messy transition from communism to free markets is an example of what Kevin Kelly called the "non-immediate" nature of emergent systems. They take time to develop and grow. Leaders can facilitate this growth like a gardener would by creating the correct environment, but they cannot command the process to accelerate any more than a gardener can command a tomato plant to produce fruit.

THINK OF PROCESSES, NOT PRODUCTS

One way to increase our tolerance of the messiness often necessary to facilitate emergent order is to get comfortable with process thinking. We tend to view the world as made up of objects or outcomes and we focus on their static nature. But if we focus on processes this can help us accept some messiness as a foundation for order.

Look around you. You may be sitting in a chair, holding a book. Perhaps your pet is nearby and your coffee mug is perched on the side table. All the objects around you can be viewed not just as items but as processes, as a series of changes that happen over time. When we name or identify a thing, we focus on its current nature: my coffee, my pet, that chair. But by naming it, we also presume its existence over time, since there is no need to name something that you will never reference in the future. And when that future comes, the named thing will have changed. This is true of inanimate objects, but it is especially true of living things. All things change, even though they do not change all at once. I ingest food, the material that makes up my body changes over time, but I continue to exist as a recognizable process. A sapling grows into a great oak; it is the same tree but very different. A river very visibly and constantly changes but also remains recognizable enough to plot it on a map. Yet when a named thing changes enough, we may no longer use the name we had assigned it. What was water is now ice; what was a cupcake is now an extra centimeter around my waist; what was an egg became a chicken and now is cordon bleu.

Perhaps this seems an unnecessarily convoluted way to think about the world but emphasizing the process view can help us realize a few things. Most importantly, thinking in processes emphasizes that each process has a history of which we may not be aware, but which may influence its future. Recall the concept of anti-reductionism from Chapter Three. The history of many processes is irreducible—we cannot summarize it easily. This is particularly true of systems that exhibit emergent order, such as living organisms, economies, or ecosystems. A snapshot of the current state of such systems cannot predict their futures because the systems are more than the sum of their current components. Think back to the example of the wave in a stadium. To someone who had never experienced the phenomenon, a single picture of a wave in progress would not at all explain what was happening. But that picture, plus a description of the simple rules that everyone was following—the process—would enable the observer to better understand what would happen next.

Focusing on processes also helps reinforce that change is inevitable, even to objects that seem permanent. Iron will rust; stone will crumble; even diamonds are not forever. If you're too focused on how things are, you may misjudge what they will become. Thinking of the world around us as made up of processes also reveals the interconnectedness of what often seem like discrete things. In particular, it can help us appreciate how our actions shape the things and people we interact with—and how they shape us.

In short, seeing processes rather than things helps us take a more connected, dynamic, and emergent view of the world, which often is the more realistic view. This can help us tolerate some messiness and better avoid the illusion of control.

CONCLUSION

Leadership without control is not only possible, but it is the way things always have been. Thinking that leaders are in control is part of what General McChrystal calls "the mythology of leadership" in his book *Leaders: Myth and Reality*.[146] As new technology and an ever more complex world dispel this illusion, successful leaders will embrace reality and with it open themselves to the powerful opportunity to better facilitate productive emergent orders.

I cannot put it better than General McChrystal did in an interview about his book: "Leadership is really an emergent property of complex systems, arising from the learning and collaboration among leaders and followers."[147] Emergent leaders will search for emergent solutions to emergent problems, embrace the messiness necessary to facilitate emergent order, and think in terms of processes, not outcomes or products.

146 Stanley McChrystal, *Leaders: Myth and Reality*, (Portfolio, 2018), 7.
147 Brook Manville, "Why Leadership Can't Be All About You," *Forbes*, July 28, 2019.

CHAPTER 6

Your Role in Emergent Systems

"[T]he brain fools the mind into believing it is in control."

— VERNON L. SMITH, "CONSTRUCTIVIST AND
ECOLOGICAL RATIONALITY IN ECONOMICS"
(PARAPHRASING MICHAEL S. GAZZANIGA)

Have you ever used an old-fashioned hourglass, one with two glass bulbs filled with sand and connected by a narrow pipe through which the sand can pass one grain at a time? This narrow pipe, the neck of the glass, is what makes the hourglass work. Above and below that point, the sand is scattered. If you shake the hourglass, you can rearrange the grains of sand in endless ways. But grains of sand always move through the pipe the same way: one at a time. As a grain of sand moves toward the neck, toward that constraint, its path becomes more predictable until, as it passes through the neck, only one path is possible. And then it collides with grains of sand in the lower bulb, and the possible paths multiply.

I like to think of my consciousness as sitting at the neck of a giant metaphorical hourglass. This narrow channel is where I experience the effects of many different emergent systems, and it is within this narrow channel that I make decisions that contribute to these systems.

Recall that in Chapter Three we discussed how emergent systems are often built up from other, smaller emergent systems, creating a hierarchy of systems, each with their own borders that filter and admit signals. Our bodies are an example of this, composed as they are of smaller, bounded systems of emergent order. And each of us are part of larger systems of emergent order. The "smaller-than-human" systems that you call your body and your brain are a unique form of emergent order that has become self-aware. These systems *are* you but can also be affected by your choices. And you yourself are also a participant in many emergent systems, such as your family, your neighborhood, and your society. Your choices affect both the "smaller-than-human" systems of your body and brain as well as these "bigger-than-human" systems. In either case, your choices take place at that narrow neck of the hourglass. The signals generated by your choices are like grains of sand passing through the neck—the further removed from that passageway, the less predictable their impact.

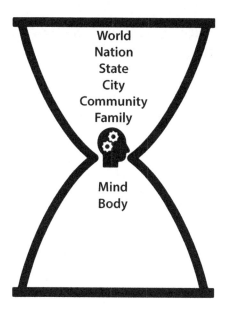

World
Nation
State
City
Community
Family

Mind
Body

You therefore relate to emergent systems from two different perspectives. You metaphorically "look down" on the smaller-than-human systems. Your decisions affect these systems from outside their boundaries with a bird's eye sense of perspective but lacking fine details—and we know that in complex systems, the fine details can make an enormous difference. For bigger-than-human systems, you metaphorically "look up" from the bottom, from within the bounds of your family and your community. Your actions feed into the system. You *are* a detail and, as such, the signals you send are part of the processing of the system.

To better understand these two different perspectives, let's look at what is similar between two selected categories of emergent systems, one from each bell of the hourglass: companies and your body.

FIRMS: ISLANDS OF PLANNING IN AN OCEAN OF EMERGENCE

Economists have long examined why companies exist. Economists study systems of exchange and the order that emerges when people individually seek to make the best deal they can to get the resources they need to pursue their objectives. The simplest exchanges are one-time marketplace trades between individuals; some of my apples for some of your oranges, for example.

But most commercial activity isn't between two individuals. Most commerce is between an individual and a company, or between two companies. Companies typically don't use markets internally. If I need a computer to do my job, I don't individually negotiate the price with my IT department. Within companies, co-ops, nonprofits, voluntary associations, and many other types of organizations, the internal interactions are governed by planning and hierarchy, not marketplace exchanges. Companies are like islands of non-market cooperation in an ocean of market exchange.[148]

Why do these islands form and why do they take the shapes they do?

One of the clearest answers was offered by economist Ronald Coase in a paper entitled "The Nature of the Firm."[149] His basic answer was transactions costs. Transactions costs are the costs (in time and money) incurred to make an exchange

---

148 Ronald Coase, "The Nature of the Firm," *Economia*, 4 no. 16, (1937), 388 (quoting D.H. Robertson who refers to firms as "islands of conscious power in this ocean of unconscious co-operation...").

149 Ibid. 386 – 405.

happen. You can think of them as drag on trade, like the friction of water on a boat's hull. For example, when you go to the store to buy a box of pencils, you aren't just paying for the pencils. There are other costs. You have to travel to the store. You must search the store for office supplies section and then pick the right brand and style. You have to wait in the checkout line. You have to clumsily count out money or try to figure out how to swipe your card. Similarly, store incurs costs when selling you those pencils. The store must pay rent; they must maintain a clean, orderly, and well-stocked store; and they must pay the cashier. Similarly, there are costs to transport the pencils from the factory where they were produced to the store where you are buying them. All of these costs are tangential to the actual costs to produce pencils, but they are necessary to facilitate the transaction of selling pencils to you.

One easy way to reduce transactions' costs is to reduce the number of transactions by bundling them. For example, you probably don't take separate trips to the grocery store to buy each different item you need. Most people make up a list and go once or twice a week. Similarly, if you end up going through the cashier's line multiple times, it is because you forgot something—not because you wanted to incur those transaction costs multiple times. Stores could, in theory, hire a new set of cashiers every day, every hour, or even for every new customer, but it's simply easier for both the store and the cashier to hire a permanent staff to fulfill the same need over and over.

Bundling transactions requires planning and prediction. When a grocery store hires cashiers, it has to guess as to how many customers it will have in the future. It is very unlikely to get this guess perfectly right, meaning it will almost certainly waste money paying idle cashiers or lose money by having too few cashiers to handle demand. But if these losses are less than the transactions costs to structure the relationship with cashiers a different way, then the store will prefer to hire permanent cashiers.

This was Coase's basic insight: Companies form in part to reduce transactions costs. Firms take a risk by trading the robustness and flexibility of pure market transactions for increased efficiency of planning, bundling services together in a cost-effective manner. In fact, one dimension on which corporations compete is reducing transactions costs so they can deliver a product or service cheaper than their competitor. (There are even consulting firms that sell advice to other firms about how to refine their processes to reduce transactions costs.)

Even though corporations have more coordinated planning than pure markets, they still are collective endeavors of autonomous individuals. As such, corporations exhibit internal emergent phenomena. Such emergence isn't through market mechanisms, but through shared corporate culture, soft skills, and embedded knowledge. As we discussed in Chapter Five, these phenomena are often critical to a company's goals and missions, but they cannot be strictly controlled or designed by company leadership. Because of these emergent phenomena, CEOs grapple with their own Hayekian knowledge problem (see Chapter Seven) when trying to steer their companies. Successful corporate leaders foster an environment that capitalizes on the emergent orders within their companies; less successful corporate leaders often struggle against these phenomena.

TOURING DIFFERENT ISLANDS

Coase's insight helps us understand why and where we see top-down control blended with emergent phenomena. But not all organizations are the same, and we can learn something about the power of emergence by comparing the structure and evolution of different institutions. Let's look at two examples.

Could there be two large organizations more different than the United States Department of Veterans Affairs—a giant government agency with, to be honest, not a great reputation for innovation—and Amazon, one of the most innovative private companies in the world? My friend Paul (not his real name) has worked at both and has seen how the two organizations deal with complexity differently. "The public/private distinction doesn't matter," he told me. "They are both big and things get messy and hard to find." But maybe the messes are different?

The Department of Veterans Affairs is a very large and complicated organization. It runs the Veterans Health Administration, which is the largest integrated health care network in the United States (1,255 health care facilities serving nine million enrolled veterans each year)—and that's just one of its four missions.[150] Its headquarters in Northwest DC

---

150 "About VA," U.S. Department of Veterans Affairs, accessed February 24, 2021.

is a nondescript government building save for the fact that there is back-in only parking in front. To manage its more than 350,000 employees, it has a byzantine administrative structure. Twenty-three different "offices" of staff support three separate administrations, each with their own undersecretary. The *2019 Functional Organization Manual*, which describes the "organization structures, missions, tasks, and authorities" of the VA, is 460 mind-numbing pages.[151] Hierarchy abounds.

Paul knows that hierarchy well, having worked as a VA attorney for more than eight years, including in the VA's Board of Veteran Appeals which reviews and decides veterans' benefit appeals that have been declined at lower levels of the complex benefits process. Despite—or perhaps because of—all the hierarchy and organization design, it can be difficult to find the right person to talk to at the VA. Veterans who have concerns about benefits have an entire office dedicated to helping them navigate through the process, but many still hire private attorneys to help them find their way. There is an enormous backlog of cases, some of which have been in process for more than a decade.

But changing procedures at the VA is very difficult. Leadership, which is frequently hauled up before Congress to testify, is very risk-averse. As a result, even minor tweaks to procedures needs to go through many levels of approval. Change at the VA is glacial, even though many agree on the need for change. Bipartisan VA reform proposals make frequent

---

151 "Functional Organizational Manual," Department of Veterans Affairs, accessed February 24, 2021.

appearances in Congress, usually after some precipitating news event involving veterans. But substantial reform is infrequent at best. For Paul, having repeatedly seen proposed reforms ignore the functional realities of the VA, such efforts sparked skepticism of any real productive change.

Paul now works at Amazon Web Services, a subsidiary of Amazon, where he helps manage solutions for government customers. In some ways, he tells me, the VA and Amazon are similar. Like the VA, Amazon is a very large and complex organization. The company employs over eight hundred thousand people, making it the second-largest private employer in the United States after Walmart. Amazon has a diverse array of business units, including grocery stores, an e-commerce platform, cloud computing services, consumer products, medicine delivery, and artificial intelligence services. In 2019, Amazon earned over $200 billion in sales and its market valuation at one point reached $1 trillion.[152] While the company began as an online bookseller without any physical presence, it currently maintains over 175 fulfillment warehouses around the world and seven different types of physical retail stores.[153]

Paul tells me that it can also be difficult to find the right person to talk to at Amazon. Amazon takes a decentralized approach to management. They are famous for their "two-pizza team" limit, where no project team can be bigger than the number of people who could be fed by two pizzas. These

---

152 Daniel Sparks, "Amazon's Record 2019 in 7 Metrics," *Motley Fool* (February 6, 2020).

153 Patrick Sisson, "Amazon's bonkers warehouse and delivery empire, by the numbers," *Curbed*, (November 26, 2019).

teams have a lot of autonomy. They are empowered to elevate any concerns as high as they need to accomplish their goals. Teams are also encouraged to build their own solutions. For example, Paul built for his team a tool to track client contacts. According to Paul, this autonomy is empowering, but can be wasteful. The decentralized structure means it can be very hard to find out who does what. And it leads to a lot of duplicated effort. After all, many teams at Amazon need to track contacts with clients; wouldn't it be easier to just have one system for all those teams to use? "People think government is inefficient," Paul explained. "My Amazon team has transitioned through five different project management systems in the last year."

Paul described the typical problem this way:

> "You know that XKCD cartoon, the one about many different USB standards? 'These fourteen standards are a mess! Let's replace them and do it right this time. Now there are fifteen standards, what a mess!' At Amazon (and probably at every tech company), it's common that people can't find exactly the right tool for some job. There are several tools that are 80 percent right for the job, but that's not enough. So they build it themselves. Except when they're about 80 percent of the way done they get distracted by something else. Now there's yet another 80 percent tool that the next person will have to sort through. It's this morass of many different training portals and knowledge management portals. And from that perspective, it looks a lot like the federal government. I guess I'm very used to living professionally in these very large organizations where you've got

an endless wiki that isn't actually maintained, and at
some point somebody says, 'Oh geez, we should just
build a page that documents all of the resources for
problem x,' and it turns out somebody already did that
two years ago but then obviously stopped maintaining
it the day they finished building it."[154]

So both the VA and Amazon are large, complex organizations. They can even feel similarly frustrating for workers trying to accomplish things within them. But the results are very different. Amazon is adaptive, evolutionary, and benefits consumers in a way that I am sure the VA would love to duplicate but cannot. What makes these organizations so different?

For Paul, the difference is typified by the leadership attitudes toward autonomy, empowering and trusting employees. As mentioned, Amazon strongly encourages teams and individuals to do whatever it takes to solve problems, including building their own systems—even if such independence looks duplicative or wasteful from the outside. Amazon pushes decision-making down to teams. They see this decentralization as a strength. Pushing decision-making down enables emergent order across the company. Teams can focus on solving the specific problems they face rather than trying to design generalizable solutions. Even so, those many duplicative 80 percent finished products aren't as wasteful as they might seem. Several of them have, after many iterations and adaptions, evolved into useful and profitable products.

---

154 The cartoon that Paul is referring to is here: "A Webcomic of Romance, Sarcasm, Math, and Language, xkcd, accessed April 6, 2021.

The most famous is Amazon Web Services, a powerful cloud computing platform that started as an internal tool for the Amazon shopping platform.

What about the VA? "My impression is that leadership at the VA looks at autonomy as a risk," Paul told me. "They worry what crazy thing some individual might do"; hence many levels of approval for changes and slow adaptation, if any. Reforms, when attempted, are large-scale and driven from the top down. This approach may limit certain kinds of risk. But it also stifles emergent order. With the complex and incredibly important set of problems the VA is attempting to address, it needs to embrace a little bit of messiness in order to free up the system to evolve.

In addition to cultural differences—and perhaps explaining those cultural differences—there is one other big difference between Amazon and the VA. Returning to Coase, Amazon faces swift penalties for unnecessary costs, unlike the VA. If Amazon is unnecessarily inefficient, messy, or bureaucratic, it misses out on profits and it gives its competitors the opportunity to gain market share. The VA faces weaker and different incentives. As a government agency, it lacks competitors, and it is not necessarily rewarded for efficiency or efficacy.

RESHAPING BOUNDARIES

In the terms of emergent systems that we learned about in Chapter Three, Coase's transaction costs are signals and the separation of a company from the market is a boundary. Transactions costs are very specific kind of signal that drives organizations to adjust boundaries. Outside of the organization, new technology or business practices can change transactions costs, and this puts pressure on organizational boundaries to evolve. For example, most small merchants used to maintain their own inventory and handle their own shipping. But specialized companies like Amazon and Shopify offer such services inexpensively enough that it no longer makes sense for many companies to keep those functions in-house. Today, when you buy a product from an Instagram ad, chances are that Shopify handled the payment, packaging, and shipping on behalf of the merchant.

Changes in transaction costs can also generate entirely new business models. For example, the smartphone reduced the cost to connect a person needing a ride with someone willing to drive them, making it possible for an app like Uber or Lyft to arrange such rides on the fly.

In Chapter Five, Professor Peter Boettke explained that "emergent order comes from emergent messes." Both the VA and Amazon have complex structures that even insiders might describe as "messy." Both are difficult to deal with and bring challenges to insiders and outsiders. But Amazon's structure of pushing decision-making down to the local level is better at fostering emergent order out of the mess because it enables the organization to react to market signals more adeptly.

Firms like Amazon and the VA are just some of the many emergent institutions that make up our society. Other important emergent institutions include churches, schools, local government, book clubs, and families. These institutions form the many different communities in which we participate. Unlike Amazon, these non-commercial organizations don't necessarily have financial motives. But they still compete for scarce resources and therefore are shaped by a combination of those pressures and the effect of transaction costs.

Let me share a personal example of how changed external pressures can shape even informal institutions. I have a group of close friends from law school. We're scattered all over the country. Every two years or so we get together for a weekend in a city that none of us live in just to hang out and catch up. Historically, other than that weekend, we have pretty much communicated through the occasional group text. Why? We're all busy with family, jobs, and local friends. Yet COVID turned that on its head. When getting together via Zoom is the only way to hang out, it doesn't matter if those friends are next door or across the country. Thus, arranging a meeting with some of my oldest friends was suddenly as easy as "meeting up" with my friends who just happened to live nearby. The technology and the transaction costs had changed. The result? A standing weekly Zoom with my law school friends. I now talk weekly to people that I used to see only every other year. The shape of that social institution has changed because of the change in transaction costs and the payoffs relative to other options.

Similarly, other social institutions—everything from churches to corporations—constantly change their boundaries depending on the conditions around them, including transaction costs. We'll learn more about how you can assist those changes in Chapter Ten and how those changes can shape you in Chapter Eleven.

YOUR BOUNDARIES

In a very general way, the human body is like Amazon or the VA. Each body is a collection of different parts that cooperate to form a whole, with a boundary that distinguishes it from everything around it. The boundary between us and our environment, like the boundary between a company and the market, is porous and dynamic but widely recognizable. A banana on the counter or a book on a shelf is not me; if I consume either, it can become part of me, just as the thoughts I write down or speak aloud can become a part of someone else. Even as the physical matter and ideas that make us up shift over time, we still recognize a boundary between ourselves and the world. Similarly, a company that hires and fires, sells off divisions, or acquires new lines of business still maintains a recognizable boundary between itself and the market.

As explained previously, changes to transaction costs can reshape the company/market boundary. A similar phenomenon shapes the boundary between an organism and the environment. Competing for limited resources in its ecological niche drives what functions are clustered in an organism and which are not. Could humans have six hearts and four eyes and night vision? Maybe, and in some ways that could be better. But under evolutionary pressure and competition for resources, the current configuration emerged as the most suitable solution to date.

So, what does this imply for our bodies? A company might outsource its shipping department. But it seems unlikely that we'll outsource our arms or our legs any time soon. And in one way, that's correct—the fundamental physics and biology that determine how much energy our limbs need to work don't change nearly as fast as the technologies that affect companies' transaction costs. The boundaries of our physical bodies probably will not change anytime soon.

But, in a very real way, we outsource our body's functions all the time. I use a hammer rather than my fist to pound a nail. I cut my steak with a knife rather than chewing off hunks with my teeth. I ride my bike or drive my car rather than walk to the store. This type of outsourcing is also increasingly common for mental work. I don't bother memorizing everyone's phone number when I can put it in my smartphone. More and more, people are seeking tools and techniques for "personal information management"—one popular online course even calls this "Building a Second Brain."[155]

We outsource our body's functions, and we gain a lot by doing so. But the key takeaway from our discussion of transactions costs is to remember that shifting the "costs" by employing new tools and techniques will change the shape of our lives, just like changed transaction costs can remake a company or even an entire industry. When we consider employing new tools—or simply using the ones nature has provided us—we can benefit from using our CEO-like position of overseeing (although not necessarily controlling) our bodies and our chosen augments. We can consciously step back and evaluate how such tools have consumed our time and energy and how the cost of switching to new tools will measure up against

---

155 "Building A Second Brain FAQ," Building A Second Brain, accessed April 1, 2021.

the benefits of such tools. We'll talk more about these lessons in Chapter Nine.

CONCLUSION

You sit at an intersection between emergent systems. You are a self-aware emergent system, and you are part of many larger emergent systems. Sitting at this intersection, your choices influence all of these emergent systems. The larger the system, the less influence you exercise over its total shape. This may seem like a weak position, but it is not. The choices you make will shape you, your community, and your world. The rest of this book is about how to make the most of your choices in our complex world.

CHAPTER 7

Emergent Leadership in Public Policy

___

"[I]t seems to have been reserved to the people of this country to decide, by their conduct and example, the important question, whether societies of men are really capable or not, of establishing good government from reflection and choice, or whether they are forever destined to depend, for their political constitutions, on accident and force."

— ALEXANDER HAMILTON, FEDERALIST PAPERS: NO. 1[156]

On either side of the Federal Trade Commission building in Washington, DC, stand two massive Art Deco statues. Each looming twelve-foot-tall limestone piece depicts a hulking man wresting a powerful horse by the bridle. These statues, together titled "Man Controlling Trade," were intended to symbolize the mission of the FTC. The agency, created in

---

156 Alexander Hamilton, Federalist No. 1, in *Federalist Papers: Primary Documents in American History.* Library of Congress. Accessed April 9, 2021.

1914, is the primary federal agency in charge of consumer protection and one of two agencies charged with enforcing US antitrust laws. It was created as part of President Woodrow Wilson's progressive effort to move the task of governance into expert agencies, independent from political pressure.[157]

I worked at the Federal Trade Commission for four years. The seven-story wedged-shaped building (on a map it looks like a piece of candy corn) is physically at the center of the federal government—it sits almost exactly halfway between the White House and the US Capitol. The Supreme Court is less than a mile away. Surrounded by the three branches of government, I walked past "Man Controlling Trade" each day.

It made me wonder: Is that the purpose of government? To control the complex systems of human society?

The words "control" and "government" are linguistically linked. The term "govern" comes from the Greek word "kubernan," which literally means "to steer or pilot a ship."[158] Linguistically, then, government is the system that seeks to steer a group of people—a town, city, state, or country, for example—controlling its path as if it were a ship on the ocean.

I have problems with that metaphor. It imagines government as something separate and outside of society, even though leaders in government are necessarily a part of society. If society is a ship, it is a very strange ship comprised of many

---

157 "Our History: Federal Trade Commission," Federal Trade Commission, accessed February 24, 2021.

158 "govern," Online Etymology Dictionary, accessed March 1, 2021.

pilots who interact with each other. It is a complex system, and any "steering" is an emergent result of those interactions.

As a result, government leaders and others who seek to shape public policy could benefit enormously from a better understanding of emergent order. During my time at the FTC, I experienced the challenges of attempting to steer complex systems and learned from others who had spent much larger portions of their professional lives in government service. My experience at the FTC showed me that understanding emergent order is vital to the work of governing for at least three reasons.

- **First, emergent order is a part of the world to be governed.** Government interacts with the physical and social world, both of which are full of emergent order. Some of these emergent orders are hugely beneficial. Others are damaging and might even lead to calls for government regulation and control. Recognizing emergent phenomenon and understanding what conditions stifle it and what encourage it will better help government achieve its goals.
- **Second, understanding emergent order helps government focus its efforts where it is most effective.** Understanding what can be controlled, what cannot be controlled, and what side effects might occur will enable government to focus its resources where they can make the most positive difference. Rather than be King Canute trying to issue commands to the ocean tides, understanding emergent order can help government officials pursue their initiatives in sync with the tides.
- **Third, governments themselves exhibit emergent order.** Governments are created by, constituted of, and

(ideally) serve human beings. Like all joint, sustained efforts of individuals, governments exhibit emergent behavior. Government leaders might wish to believe that, unlike the ant queen, they are fully in control of the organizations they head. But government isn't only shaped by those who participate in it and those who it serves—it also shapes those people. Understanding the existence of such feedback loops is key to understanding how to lead in government effectively.

As we'll discuss below, because government leaders seek to control a world filled with emergent systems, they face a fundamental knowledge problem that limits their potential effectiveness as compared to more bottom up, emergent solutions. The government leader who is aware of the knowledge problem and other effects of emergent order can focus government action where it is most useful. Key to navigating the knowledge problem is an attitude of regulatory humility, which will help public policy leaders be aware of emergent order and account for it in their plans—or help them realize when planning simply isn't appropriate.

THE KEY LEADERSHIP CHALLENGE: ACKNOWLEDGE THE KNOWLEDGE PROBLEM

Policymakers seek to govern complex systems that exhibit emergent order. Reasonable regulation requires information about the existing and future state of society, industry, or technology. And yet, because they seek to regulate complex systems, regulators cannot gather all the relevant information for three reasons.

First, the necessary knowledge in an emergent system is dispersed. We talked earlier about how no one person knows everything necessary to manufacture a pencil. The knowledge to produce that simple technology is spread among millions of people across the globe. A regulator seeking to govern pencil manufacturing cannot gather all that information. Complicating things further, important information is also spread across time. Any rules that a regulator adopts will apply to future activities as well, but that information cannot be gathered by the regulator making the rules now. Thus, a regulator must anticipate future changes. That's an impossible job even for industry participants. Markets and other emergent systems create information as part of their operation. If the single best way to produce pencils was already known, competition would be unnecessary. But, as Hayek has explained, market competition is the procedure for discovering the relevant information to improve, for example, the production of pencils.[159] Because information is dispersed geographically and temporally, there is much information that will never be accessible to the regulator.

Second, much relevant knowledge in an emergent system is latent, meaning it cannot be described to another party. This is true at the individual level: there are many tasks that we complete that we would not be able to write down or accurately describe to another person. Think of something like riding a bike: step-by-step written instructions would be of limited use to a new rider. One learns to ride a bike

---

159 Friedrich Hayek, "Competition as a Discovery Process," *Quarterly Journal of Economics*, 5 no. 3, (2002).

by experience. Like biking, we cannot fully describe many of our physical tasks. But this is also true of many mental tasks. Ask a speechwriter how they get ideas or what they do to write a first draft, or a salesperson how they know which customers are likely to purchase and which are not, and they will only be able to tell you in the broadest terms. Because their knowledge is embedded in the complex system of their brain, the best way they can summarize how to complete such a task is simply to do it. Other examples of latent knowledge include the "soft skills" of international diplomacy or leading a company.

Complex systems have information that is latent not just at the individual level, however. Much information is latent in the connections between the individual pieces. Think of what people mean when they say "the culture of a workplace" or best practices. If you've ever read through an employee handbook, you know there is always a significant difference between what is contained within the handbook and how things actually work. That gap is latent information that the company cannot successfully document. Imagine how much harder it would be for an outside regulator.

Political scientist and anthropologist James C. Scott uses the term *mētis* to describe latent information that isn't expressible even by the person or organization most expert in the relevant task.[160] Most human endeavors include significant amounts of *mētis*. If not even the expert entity performing the task knows how to accurately describe how they do it, a regulator has little hope of gathering such information.

---

160 James C. Scott, *Seeing Like A State*, (Yale University Press, 1998) 6.

Third and finally, much of the collectable information cannot be summarized without losing essential content. It is irreducible. Physicists can predict the swing of a pendulum without having to calculate the motion of all the individual atoms because the average of all those individual elements captures the important and necessary information. And to the extent the average is off by a little bit, the result will also only be off by a little bit. But for complex systems, a small initial inaccuracy can lead to a widely divergent result. Furthermore, in a complex system, like those that involve human choices, the relationships between the elements are what matters. These relationships cannot be "averaged" without losing the important information. Imagine averaging the beliefs and desires of one person with the very different beliefs and desires of another; the result would not give an accurate representation of either person's views. In fact, people very often hold positions that contradict each other and possibly even themselves. The interaction between people acting on different views over time is what generates information, as discussed above. Summarizing conflicting views does not produce the needed information and eliminates the possibility of doing so.

Scott would say that knowledge that is dispersed, latent, or irreducible—each common in complex systems—is *illegible* to the regulator; the regulator cannot read it.[161] This limits the regulator's ability to regulate effectively.

---

161 James C. Scott, *Seeing Like A State*, (Yale University Press, 1998), 2.

IMPOSED LEGIBILITY DOESN'T SOLVE THE KNOWLEDGE PROBLEM AND CREATES NEW PROBLEMS

But few regulators acknowledge the knowledge problem, as Scott points out in *Seeing Like A State*. Government officials rarely resign themselves to the fact that important information is illegible to them. Scott provides many examples of central authorities' efforts to impose legibility on situations that they seek to govern. Such examples include standardized weights and measures, mandatory surnames, property surveys and population registers, scientific agriculture, and design of cities.

When a regulator imposes legibility, they do so in pursuit of a specific objective: easing tax collection, maximizing crops, or streamlining military transportation. Often states impose legibility to assemble a summarized simplified view to guide interventions. Scott describes such efforts to make things "more legible—and hence manipulable—from above and from the center."[162]

When legibility is imposed for a purpose, it necessarily simplifies and fails to fully capture the local knowledge it summarizes. Scott describes this as "rather like abridged maps [that] did not successfully represent the actual activity of the society they depicted, nor were they intended to; they represented only that slice of it that interested the official observer."[163] *Mētis* in particular is often discarded when governments collect information. Often, those imposing legibility mistakenly regarding *mētis* as useless noise or disorder when it actually represents complexity.

---

162 Ibid. 2.
163 Ibid. 3.

As Scott describes, instruments of imposed legibility such as censuses, surveys, and population registers have long been the basic tools of government. As governments gathers information, even simplified information, it can more precisely and effectively deliver services and pursue its mandates. But as its mandates and purposes grow, so too does its need for information and thus its need for increased legibility. In some cases, when a state imposes legibility, it may disrupt a local community and therefore increase the perceived need for the centralized authority to intervene, in a self-fulfilling prophecy. For these reasons, as regulators gather information, they can experience what data scientist Nate Silver has described as "[o]ne of the pervasive risks that we face in the information age... even if the amount of knowledge in the world is increasing, the gap between what we know and what we think we know may be widening."[164]

In other words, if regulators are not mindful of the knowledge problem, they can start to mistake the map they've developed for the territory they are regulating.

Even worse, attempts to mitigate the knowledge problem may distort the real world, eliminating useful emergent order mechanisms simply because the regulators are focused on their particular regulatory need. Scott tells the story of German forestry science, which emerged as a scientific effort by the German government to maximize the productivity of forests. Scientists started with simple efforts to measure output of commercial wood over time. But those measurements

---

164 Nate Silver, *The Signal and the Noise: Why So Many Predictions Fail - but Some Don't*, (Penguin Group, 2012), 45.

became the narrow lens through which the government saw these forests. That in turn prompted efforts to reshape the forests to be more easily measured. Within just a generation, the complex, diverse, and messy old-growth forests were replaced with orderly, uniform forests planted on a grid—convenient, aesthetically pleasing, and manipulable. Output of commercial wood soared.

But there were serious downsides. "The monocropped forest was a disaster for peasants who were now deprived of all the grazing, food, raw materials, and medicines that the earlier forest ecology had afforded," Scott explains. Ironically, the newly legible forests also disrupted a complicated ecological process of soil generation and became more vulnerable to pests. Ultimately, the legible forests experienced a steep decline in output of commercial wood.[165]

As Scott summarizes, this story "illustrates the dangers of dismembering an exceptionally complex and poorly understood set of relations and processes in order to isolate a single element of instrumental value,"—in that case, commercial wood output.[166] Regulators who forge ahead with ambitious plans without acknowledging the knowledge problem risk similar failure.

THE KNOWLEDGE PROBLEM GUIDES WHERE GOVERNMENT SHOULD ACT

The knowledge problem does not mean that regulators can gather no useful information and can do nothing. They

---

165 James C. Scott, *Seeing Like A State*, (Yale University Press, 1998), 14-21.
166 James C. Scott, *Seeing Like A State*, (Yale University Press, 1998), 21.

obviously can gather useful knowledge. Often it is possible to do so without imposing the worst consequences of forced legibility. But ultimately, policymakers face real constraints on the amount of information they can gather and centralize. The practical result is that centralized policy makers are working with far less information than the distributed, emergent systems they seek to control. They need to acknowledge and manage this tradeoff.

This reduced information might be fine in some cases. It might be that not all the information is needed for the specific regulatory purpose. Or it may be that the relevant information is easier to gather in some cases than in others. This is more likely to be true in areas that change slowly and incrementally. For example, understanding the dynamics of a slow-changing and long-established industry such as coal mining is more easily done than for a fast-evolving industry such as cryptocurrency.

It also might be that the policymaker faced with a particular problem has no choice other than to forge ahead without all the important information. It could even be that the problem itself is an emergent result, such as the beach in Buchanan's story.

Government isn't the only arena in which leaders must make decisions with far less than perfect information. My point is not that government leaders should do nothing unless they have perfect information. But leaders in government can focus their energies and resources most productively when they are aware of the knowledge problem.

THE FUNDAMENTAL ATTITUDE: REGULATORY HUMILITY

The knowledge problem and the need for messiness talked about earlier serve as foundational constraints on what it is possible for government or other centralized organizations to accomplish. When faced with these limits, the proper response is one of humility. Yet not many top regulators are known for their humility. High profile government jobs often draw people with egos to match.

Maureen K. Ohlhausen certainly has achievements that would justify a big ego. After more than a decade at the Federal Trade Commission in a variety of leadership roles and a stint in the private sector, she was appointed by President Obama to serve as a Commissioner at the Federal Trade Commission. Under President Trump she became the acting chairman of the agency, a position she held for fifteen months. She led efforts to reduce the burdens of occupational licensing—a type of bureaucratic red tape that often keeps those trying to climb the ladder of success from reaching even the first rung. She has published dozens of book chapters, law review articles, essays and op-eds, and given countless public speeches. Ohlhausen now chairs the global antitrust and competition practice of international law firm Baker Botts. She is a heavy hitter in antitrust and consumer protection law on the substance but has also been praised for her ability to "move the needle" by persuading people to her position. Another former FTC chairman once compared her to Eisenhower in her ability to pick a direction and bring disagreeing parties together to move in that direction.

Ohlhausen is also known not just as one of the most capable people in DC, but also as one of the most humble. I spent my entire time at the FTC working directly for acting Chairman Ohlhausen, first as an attorney advisor in her office and then as the agency's acting chief technologist. I saw her treat her staff, her fellow Commissioners, other FTC employees, and even defendants whom the FTC was suing with respect and engage them with an open mind, seeking to learn from them. She took her job seriously but didn't take herself too seriously. I remember her often quoting HBO comedy *Veep* to capture some of the absurdities of Washington, DC, politics.

Humility is a part of Ohlhausen's character, but it is also a part of her regulatory philosophy. She has long advocated for *regulatory humility*, which she describes as "recognizing the inherent limitations of regulation and acting in accordance with those limitations."

Regulatory humility also means acknowledging what Ohlhausen has called "the Procrustean problem with prescriptive regulation." The Greek mythological character Procrustes was a blacksmith and the son of the sea god Poseidon. Procrustes generously opened his home to weary travelers, offering them a place to stay. He even built a special iron bed just for his guests. But there was a catch. If his guest was too small for the bed, Procrustes would stretch the guest to fit. If the guest was too big, Procrustes would amputate limbs as necessary. Eventually, Procrustes met his own demise at the hands of the Greek hero Theseus, who fit Procrustes to his own bed by cutting off his head.

The lesson of this gruesome tale for regulators, according to Ohlhausen, is:

[It] warns us against the very human tendency to squeeze complicated things into simple boxes, to take complicated ideas or technologies or people and fit them into our preconceived models... [W]e often use this backward-fitting approach without recognizing that we're doing it. Even worse, sometimes we're proud of our cleverness in reducing something complicated to something simple. The lesson of Procrustes for regulators and policymakers is that we should resist the urge to oversimplify. We need to make every effort to tolerate complex phenomena and to develop institutions that are robust in the face of rapid innovation.[167]

Regulatory humility counsels against arrogantly forcing complex, emergent systems into simple regulatory boxes. It helps us see new developments without seeking to impose our preconceptions on them. As Ohlhausen has argued, "these principles apply to regulation generally, but... they are particularly critical for technology or other fast-moving industries" where new developments frequently disrupt existing business and regulatory paradigms.[168]

A leader practicing regulatory humility when faced with a problem asks not just, "What is legal for us to do," but also "What *should* we do?" It takes regulatory humility to acknowledge that in some circumstances, particularly where complex systems are involved, the actions available to a government leader may simply make a problem worse or create an entirely new problem.

---

167 Maureen K. Ohlhausen, "Remarks to the American Enterprise Institute," (American Enterprise Institute, Washington D.C., April 1, 2015): 3.
168 Ibid. 3.

REGULATORY ARROGANCE IN NOMI TECHNOLOGIES

Such was the situation for Nomi Technologies, a company that settled a case with the FTC in 2015. This small startup offered retailer clients the ability to collect and analyze aggregate data about consumer traffic in client stores. The company anonymized data so that no individual could be tracked, but clients could see aggregate patterns that would help them understand how to serve customers better. While not legally required to offer consumers an opt out (because Nomi's technology did not identify individual consumers), Nomi followed FTC best practices and offered, on its website, a global opt out from all retail locations where the technology was deployed. Thus, the company went above and beyond its legal obligations.[169]

But the FTC threated to sue the young company anyway, arguing it had also promised to permit customers to opt out in person at retail locations but hadn't successfully implemented that provision. Again, this company had no legal obligation to offer any opt out. And the FTC staff provided no evidence that any consumer who had wished to opt out was unable to do so—or suffered any other type of harm. Indeed, Nomi demonstrated that visitors to its privacy policy were able to and did use the global opt out. Still, the startup, whose fundraising had been disrupted by the FTC investigation, entered a twenty-year settlement with the FTC and was subsequently acquired by a competitor.[170]

---

169 Geoffrey Manne, "The Dark Side of the FTC's Latest Privacy Case, In the Matter of Nomi Technologies," *ICLE*, April 29, 2015.

170 Anthony Ha, "Brickstream Acquires Nomi for An In-Store Analytics Team Up," *TechCrunch*, October 29, 2014.

Ohlhausen dissented from the settlement because the FTC's action actually made things worse. The decision, she argued, "undermines the Commission's own goals of increased consumer choice and transparency of privacy practices and ... imposes a penalty far out of proportion to the non-existent consumer harm."[171] If Nomi had offered no privacy options to consumers, it never would have been in trouble with the FTC. As such, the FTC's action discouraged companies from going above and beyond their legal duties. As one observer noted, "the takeaway for most companies will be: if you do not want the FTC to come after you, do the bare-minimum on privacy."[172] The FTC could have exercised regulatory humility by warning the company about the technical violation and turned to matters where enforcement attention would have benefited consumers.

HIGH MODERNISM

The opposite of regulatory humility is what Yale anthropologist James C. Scott, mentioned earlier, calls "high modernism" in his book *Seeing Like a State*. He describes how, beginning in the mid-nineteenth century, intellectuals began to aspire to administratively reorder nature and society. Scott calls it "modernism" because adherents wished to emulate the success of the then ongoing Industrial Revolution. To them, the Industrial Revolution showed the near limitless potential of scientific and technical expertise to solve practical

---

171 Maureen Ohlhausen, "Dissenting Statement of Commissioner Maureen K. Ohlhausen In the Matter of Nomi Technologies Inc. Matter No. 1323251," Federal Trade Commission, accessed February 12, 2021.

172 Elizabeth Litten, "When Privacy Policies Should NOT Be Published - Two Lessons From the FTC's Nomi Technologies Case," Fox Rothschild, May 26, 2015.

problems—including, they thought, all kinds of social problems. "High" refers to the lofty ambition of these intellectuals. For most of human history, government's goals were modest: extract taxes, repel invaders, quell rebellion. It was a new idea that the state should seek to improve the well-being of society. High modernist plans weren't incremental or subtle. They disdained history and often sought to wipe out previous approaches and replace them with wholly reengineered solutions.

High modernist governments sought "the rational design of social order commensurate with the scientific understanding of natural laws."[173] Science solved practical problems using information discovered through tools like the microscope; high modernist governments sought to solve governance problems using information gathered through state tools. But Scott distinguishes high modernism from actual scientific practice, noting that high modernism borrowed the credibility of science and technology but really was a dogma that was "uncritical, unskeptical, and thus unscientifically optimistic about the possibilities for the comprehensive planning of human settlement and production."[174]

This blind enthusiasm for a broad scope of government and confidence in the ability of experts to shape society was shared by individuals and groups that otherwise disagreed entirely on what society should look like. It found its most abhorrent and tragic expressions in Nazi Germany and Stalinist Russia, but also undergirded more democratically

---

173 James C. Scott, *Seeing Like A State*, (Yale University Press, 1998), 4.
174 Ibid.

acceptable efforts such as Woodrow Wilson's expansion of federal administrative agencies in the US.

The high modernist mindset and its lack of regulatory humility is at its most destructive when applied to complex systems that demonstrate emergent order. The high modernists sought to apply Industrial Revolution-style science to society. But the industrial revolution was built upon mastering physical systems whose sum was the total of their parts. Systems such as the steam engine are decomposable systems; they exhibit designed order, not emergent order.

In contrast, social systems display emergent order. They are more than the sum of their parts. They have deep history and context; you cannot simply disassemble and reassemble them. They are not designed and thus cannot be redesigned.

Using reductionist approaches might work to design a steam engine but cannot work to redesign society. Where the high modernists were unconstrained, such as in Stalinist Russia, they tried to create utopia but instead generated decades of human misery. Where social norms and democratic institutions constrained them more, such as in the United States, the high modernists' failures were less obviously tragic, but the successes were often in spite of, rather than because of, their grand designs.

FOUR TACTICS FOR GOVERNMENT INTERVENTIONS INTO EMERGENT ORDERS

Government efforts that ignore the knowledge problem and arrogantly impose high modernist plans have always failed—and often do so tragically. James C. Scott distills four characteristics common to these failed efforts. First, government uses simplifying tools to increase the legibility of the system to a central authority. Second, government embraces a high modernism mindset with ambitious, overly confident, and comprehensive plans for redesigning the system. Third, government possesses enough authority and power to mandate adoption of these plans. And finally, civil society is too weak to overtly resist the imposition of the plans.[175]

Scott describes the results of government interventions that share these four characteristics as "[a]t best ... fragile and vulnerable, sustained by improvisations not foreseen by its originators. At worst, [they] wreaked untold damage in shattered lives, damaged ecosystems, and fractured or impoverished societies."[176] To avoid these consequences, Scott argues for "institutions that are instead multifunctional, plastic, diverse, and adaptable—in other words, institutions that are powerfully shaped by *mētis*."[177]

In short, Scott is calling for institutions that support and facilitate emergent order. His four characteristics of failed interventions suggests four corresponding tactics for developing "*mētis*-friendly" institutions:

- Minimize simplistic legibility
- Temper ambitious plans with prudence and humility
- Reduce the planner's ability to impose a plan

---

175 James C. Scott, *Seeing Like A State*, (Yale University Press, 1998), 4-5.
176 Ibid. 352.
177 Ibid. 353.

- Increase the ability of participants to resist or shape such plans[178]

These four tactics for government leaders are a practical application of the more general six principles of emergent mindset that I described in the introduction and discuss more fully in Chapter Twelve. For example, minimizing simplistic legibility requires humility about what is knowable as well as anticipating complicated results. Tempering ambitions plans is another way of saying be humble, stick to what you can control, and expect complicated results. Reducing the planner's ability to impose a plan is a specific form of choosing institutional constraints. And one way to increase the ability of participants to shape plans is to push decision making down to the appropriate level.

I'll elaborate on these four tactics, each of which can be applied separately or in combination with the others.

MINIMIZE SIMPLISTIC LEGIBILITY

As discussed earlier, when government seeks to understand a complex system to control it, the government increases the legibility of that system by reducing complexity. It does so by using tools such as surveys, maps, or other types of data collection. These efforts require screening out information not relevant to the government's purpose. As a

---

178 Scott briefly offers his own four rules of thumb to "make development planning less prone to disaster." He recommends taking small steps, favoring reversibility, planning on surprises by choosing flexible approaches, and planning on human inventiveness. James C. Scott, *Seeing Like A State*, (Yale University Press, 1998), 352. These overlap significantly in practical effect with the four tactics I describe.

result, when a government imposes legibility in pursuit of one purpose, it changes the system, undermining other purposes the system may have also served. Think back to the German forestry example. The old business adage that "you get what you measure" applies here. Simplistic, reductive legibility efforts to understand the system can actually damage the system.

There are two ways to minimize simplistic legibility. The most straightforward would be to avoid imposing legibility in the first place. But government leaders need certain information and insight into the system they seek to govern. Without such information, their efforts will be less effective and may fail to achieve their particular purpose.

Government can, however, choose methods of governing that need less information. Compare the relatively limited amount of information a judge needs to decide a specific case with the information needed by a legislator drafting a law that regulates an entire industry. Judges review one case or controversy at a time. The information that they need to gather is usually readily accessible from the parties involved. Their decision only directly affects the parties involved. And once the case is resolved, ongoing data reporting is typically not needed. A legislator, on the other hand, needs information from the entire industry as well as affected stakeholders. The legislation, once created, will affect all current and future industry participants. The legislation will likely require ongoing reporting or other types of transparency that will enable the government to monitor and enforce compliance. In short, case-by-case approaches typically need less information and thus reduce the need to impose legibility in order to gather relevant information. We'll talk more about case-by-case, or common law approaches, under the next tactic.

The second way to limit simplistic legibility is to avoid oversimplifying as much as possible. This is as difficult as it is obvious. In all cases, imposing legibility for one purpose affects information that could be useful for other purposes. In the worst cases, including the German forestry example and others documented by Scott, the imposed legibility destroys information necessary to carry out the state's intended purpose or otherwise undermines the intended purpose.

But while it isn't possible to completely avoid simplification, different methods of imposing legibility can be more or less harmful. Being conscious of the collateral effects of the methods by which government learns about the systems it governs can help the authority choose the least reductive model. For example, new data analysis tools may help because they can be used on complex, non-heterogenous data. Rather than squeeze needed information into a governance-friendly format, analytical tools may make it possible to collect the information in the more complex form yet still derive useful knowledge from it.

TEMPER AMBITIOUS PLANS WITH PRUDENCE AND HUMILITY
The second lesson is to avoid the high modernist mindset that seeks a top-down, usually revolutionary designed solution to the particular problem. The easiest way to avoid high modernism is to refrain from government action. Government solutions are not the only solutions. There are usually multiple competing solutions—many different answers to the problem. Such fixes could include innovative new technologies

or business models. But they could also involve non-commercial solutions such as evolving social norms, manners, or customs. And there are private agreements between parties that enable custom solutions for the specific parties involved. Finally, there is soft law, which are agreements and principles between stakeholders—sometimes including governmental entities—that are persuasive but not fully legally binding. All of this is a bit abstract now, but I will offer several concrete examples in the next chapter. The key point for now is that if a problem can be addressed by these kinds of distributed solutions, a humble regulator will step aside.

But sometimes government solutions are needed. And some lofty goals are worth pursuing. How can policy leaders avoid high modernism as they pursue such solutions and goals? How can they exercise regulatory humility, respect for the existing knowledge in the system, and realistically assess what might go wrong? Scott recommends that government leaders avoid high modernism by taking incremental steps toward their goal, allowing plenty of opportunities to receive feedback and adjust. He also encourages approaches that can be reversed without too much disturbance if things go badly.[179] Both recommendations help accommodate inevitable surprises and unanticipated reactions and adjustments that are certain to occur in a complex system.

Scott's two methods can be applied in many ways by a policymaker. But I want to highlight one often-ignored general purpose tool available to government that is both incremental and relatively easy to reverse if things go badly: common

---

179 James C. Scott, *Seeing Like a State*, (Yale University Press, 1998), 344-345.

law. I mentioned in the previous section how case-by-case approaches (of which common law is one) can minimize simplistic legibility; such approaches can also temper ambitious plans.

Common law is characterized by a judge's or other neutral decision-maker's application of general principles to individual situations.[180] Judges create common law by applying lessons from past cases (sometimes quite ancient—common law principles date back to eleventh-century England) to new situations; those new decisions will then inform other judges in future cases. Core doctrines, such as negligence or nuisance, develop over time. Those doctrines are often summarized in a judge's opinion, but they are not authoritatively written down in any one location. Instead, the law consists of the collective reasoning and conclusions of many court cases, each of which resolves a specific conflict. Each decision in a case also helps the public understand what behaviors and situations are likely to violate the law. The law therefore evolves incrementally through private litigation or government enforcement in specific cases. Analogizing to software development, common law is like the agile software development used by many phone app developers: multiple decision-makers frequently release small changes and adjust priorities as new issues arise.

Common law contrasts with statutory or legislative approach. Statutes are what most people think of when they think of "a law": a set of rules written by legislators. These rules are

---

180 Much of this section is based on an earlier version of an article I wrote for Protocol. Neil Chilson, "Why Joe Biden and Donald Trump are both wrong about Section 230." *Protocol*, November 13, 2020.

specific to the problem being tackled. They often are focused on a single industry. Such rules usually set forth obligations, responsibilities, standards for judging compliance, and punishments and remedies for noncompliance. If common law is like agile software development, statute law is more like the old waterfall methodology that developers in the 1990s commonly used: centrally managed, sequential development with infrequent releases.

For well-understood problems and slow-changing industries, statutory law can work well because the knowledge problem isn't as acute. However, even in such areas poorly designed statutes can impose unnecessary requirements that don't solve the intended problem, and outdated statutes can be difficult or counterproductive to comply with. Furthermore, statutory law rarely changes because legislation moves very slowly. Usually, such law just accumulates, unchanged, over time. Legislators' political agendas or special interests can also distort the design of statutes.

By contrast, no one designs common law—it evolves. When a court applies a principle from an earlier case, it also shapes that principle for future courts. As a result, how to comply with common law is sometimes less clear-cut. Parties often estimate it as "liability risk"—how likely are we to be sued for this? And different judges might interpret and apply the same common law principles differently.

But this ambiguity also means that over time, common law can evolve to address new problems. Common law also focuses on actual, existing problems, not theoretical or future problems. This focus means that useless common law usually fades out or is expressly eroded by court decisions over time. And special interests cannot easily distort common law because of its decentralized nature and its focus on specific conflicts rather than entire industries. Furthermore, because common law is evolutionary, it's better suited to regulating fast-moving technology than detailed legislation, which can quickly become outdated.

Rather than wait until someone is hurt by a new technology and can sue, it might seem better to pass a law ahead of time to prevent potential harms. This makes sense when Congress or a regulator understands the future path of a particular technology well and when the harms are likely to be widespread, catastrophic, and irreversible. But in most cases even experts don't understand the future of a technology very well, let alone legislators. While detailed legislation may prevent some harms, it can also prevent beneficial uses and will likely miss other harms. In such cases, it's better to address problems as they arise.

Common law better satisfies Scott's suggestions for avoiding high modernism. It is more incremental than, for example, industry-wide regulation. And the effects are concentrated on one party. If things go badly it may be too late for that particular entity, but the position can be modified for future parties.

Common law or common-law-like approaches are not the only way to temper ambitious plans, but it is one that is often overlooked.

REDUCE THE PLANNER'S ABILITY TO IMPOSE A PLAN

Another tactic is to limit the ability of the planner to impose a plan. If the planner cannot force adoption of a plan, it will need to persuade people—a process that requires compromise and emergent decision-making, and therefore incorporates a far wider range of input and knowledge.

In the private sector, forcing people to adopt a plan is difficult and potentially even illegal. Competition typically drives firms to offer attractive alternatives. Antitrust and consumer protection laws are intended to prevent the type of private power coercion that could force people to adopt a plan that they wouldn't otherwise choose. In this way, government can help reduce private planners' ability to impose a plan.

But, as the title of Scott's book *Seeing Like A State* suggests, the biggest risk of imposed plans come from the entity that holds a monopoly on legitimate force: the government. The most tragic events that Scott documents were created by governments largely unconstrained in their ability to impose plans. For example, Scott describes the Soviet government takeover and collectivization of agriculture as a "diagnostic case of authoritarian high-modernist planning ... an unprecedented transformation of agrarian life and production ... imposed by all the brute force at the state's disposal."[181] This action killed at least three to four million people and more recent figures suggest greater than twenty million people died.[182]

---

181 James C. Scott, *Seeing Like A State*, (Yale University Press, 1998), 201.
182 Ibid. 202.

The governments Scott describes had few or no limits on their authority to impose plans. Democratic states like the US tend to have constraints on the authority of government to impose central plans. In the US, such constraints include the constitutional rights of individuals, separation of powers, and federalism, to name a few. Some of these limits have eroded over time, but they remain fundamentally sound and capable of preventing the most tragic outcomes.

Even though the worst outcomes are already constrained in the US, government leaders can still evaluate various policies along this dimension. For example, when Congress considers delegating authority to an agency to address a problem, it can limit the ability of the agency to impose plans depending on the types of authority it delegates. One of the simplest examples of this would be the choice between delegating rulemaking authority to an agency rather than delegating only the ability of the agency to enforce the law congress created. The details will matter in a specific case, but generally speaking an agency with rulemaking authority is more able to impose plans on those it regulates.

In summary, government leaders who wish to foster emergent order should look for opportunities to constrain the ability of government to plan for its people.

INCREASE THE ABILITY OF THE PARTICIPANTS TO RESIST SUCH PLANS

Finally, governments (and, as we'll see in the next chapter, even companies) could improve the ability of individuals and the system to resist grand plans. Scott specifically encourages the establishment of *mētis*-friendly systems that enhance users and incorporate their values. He argues that one can test for *mētis*-friendly systems by asking, "To what degree does it promise to enhance the skills, knowledge, and responsibility of those who are a part of it?" and "How deeply [the institution] is marked by the values and experience of those who compose it?"[183] Strong and resilient systems are those that grow in concert with their participants rather than systems that are imposed upon the participants.

Democratic institutions such as elected leaders, due process rights, free speech rights, and more obscure doctrines such as jury nullification and public participation in agency rulemakings are all tools with the intent and effect of incorporating feedback into governance systems, increasing the public's ability to resist top-down plans they dislike. Most of these tools are relatively clunky and indirect. Voting, for example, occurs infrequently and rarely provides a clear signal about any one policy, as voters usually have to choose a candidate offering a bundle of policies.

The most successful ways to incorporate user input for large populations are decentralized, continuous approaches where an organization (such as a company or government) does not control the information flow. The paradigmatic example of such a system is the complex market forces that channel consumer demands into producer incentives. Such solutions can scale readily with the addition of more users. They can constantly apply a user's knowledge and values directly to the problem they are facing. And they are flexible enough to adapt to changing circumstances or user needs.

---

183 James C. Scott, *Seeing Like A State*, (Yale University Press, 1998), 353.

Government solutions inherently require centralization and will not be able to match the flexibility and comprehensive nature of distributed solutions like the prices system—hence the knowledge problem. But government approaches that leave more choices to affected individuals provide one way to let participants weigh in and resist plans with which they disagree.

* * *

These four tactics are not the complete menu of desirable policy approaches. Furthermore, each of them could be misused. For example, one could increase the ability of participants to resist government plans by, for example, calling a referendum on everything. Such direct democracy approaches magnify the zero-sum nature of politics, meaning the majority's view on any issue becomes the answer for everyone. Or, one might so limit the ability of the state to impose plans that it cannot take on any substantial projects no matter how necessary.

But these tactics can prevent the worst outcomes of government initiatives. And they give government leaders a series of criteria against which to measure various policy choices. In representative democracies like the US, policies that ignore or even distort local knowledge, offer radical change, empower forceful implementation, and reject feedback aren't going to lead to mass starvation. Yet why not offer policies that seek to understand the current system without unnecessarily disrupting it, offer incremental and reversible experiments, rely on persuasion more than mandates, and incorporate constant feedback?

CONCLUSION

"Growing up on Long Island, when we went to Jones Beach there were a million rules," Maureen Ohlhausen told me, explaining when she first realized that there can be order without someone in control. "On Jones Beach you weren't allowed to have rafts in the water. No inflatable toys. You couldn't play with a ball. And then my family moved down south. I remember the first time we went to the Outer Banks. There were practically no rules. You couldn't bring glass bottles onto the beach, but that was about it. And yet people behaved. Maybe that sounds stupid," she caveated, "but it was such a sharp contrast. It opened my eyes."

The Jones Beach regulators could have benefited from a strong dose of Ohlhausen's regulatory humility. Even the longest list of rules about beach behavior couldn't prohibit every potential risky or socially undesirable behavior that might ever occur, but it could chill a lot of fun. Could they have achieved their same goals by relying on other distributed or incremental approaches such as social norms to ensure a safe and fun environment?

Maybe, maybe not. But government leaders ought to practice regulatory humility. They should seek to mitigate their knowledge problem by choosing tools that best enable distributed, incremental solutions. Regulatory approaches ought to incorporate feedback and adapt over time. The four key tactics described above can help regulators lead with an emergent mindset. In the next chapter we'll look at specific policy areas to see how these tactics can apply to real problems.

CHAPTER 8

Case Studies

"Few things are harder to put up with than the annoyance of a good example."

— MARK TWAIN, *PUDD'NHEAD WILSON*[184]

Having laid out a structure for how emergent order can assist policymakers, I thought it would be useful to run through two examples drawn from my own past work: privacy and content moderation. These are among the most contentious issues in technology policy. Each raises difficult issues because they both deal with highly complex environments that no one fully controls. In both areas understanding emergent order is therefore helpful.

The complexity of each of these areas also means that the below discussions are neither comprehensive nor the answers definitive. Complex problems rarely have definitive solutions. Instead, my goal is to illustrate how keeping emergent order

---

184 Mark Twain, *Pudd'nhead Wilson*, (Charles L. Webster & Co., 1894), 246.

in mind can shape analysis of a particular policy problem and the types of solutions considered.

PRIVACY

Concerns about how others use information about us is as old as gossip. In the US, concerns over how government collects and uses information about its citizens are as old as the republic, with certain limitations being incorporated into the Constitution itself.

But questions about whether and how law and regulation should limit private collection and use of information about people have become unprecedently important in the information age. New technology makes data collection about individuals a ubiquitous and powerful tool. As Yale anthropologist James C. Scott (discussed in the last chapter) would explain, such technology makes certain things about the world more *legible*.

Online interactions are by design and necessity highly legible. Browsing the internet involves interactions with other people's online computers. These interactions are generally viewable by the owners of those computers and others, even if the user browses while sitting at home. For example, online advertising technology makes the path one takes across the internet more legible to deliver better targeted ads. As more of people's day-to-day activities occur online, the legibility of those activities increases. (Compare the capturable data involved when shopping on Amazon.com to shopping in your local CVS.)

Furthermore, the rise of sophisticated sensors and computational techniques means that our real-world interactions are also growing more legible. Smart sensors can detect when we arrive home or enter a retail store (see the discussion about Nomi Technologies in the previous chapter). Facial recognition technology potentially removes the relative anonymity of walking down a busy city block or drinking in a crowded bar. We shout out questions to home assistants, which use that information to improve the responses they give us.

Because our activities are more legible, some people are concerned that they are losing privacy. At the same time, we've experience mishandling of data that has harmed people, as with the millions of names and dates of birth, Social Security numbers, physical addresses, and other personal information stolen from credit rating agency Equifax—a data breach that affected more than 147 million people.[185]

WHAT IS PRIVACY?

People are increasingly concerned about privacy, but what exactly is it? Privacy is a complicated concept that many people have attempted to define, often in conflicting or incompatible ways. For our purposes here, let's define privacy very broadly as *the result of a limitation on the collection or use of information.* More specifically, a person has a degree of privacy when certain information—"private" information—about that person cannot be *perceived* or *used* by another entity. Privacy is a concept that only makes sense with respect to at least one other party. Thus, the less information about

---

185 "EPIC - Equifax Data Breach," EPIC, accessed February 24, 2021.

Bob that Carol can *perceive* or *use*, the more privacy Bob has from Carol.

The concept of privacy, as suggested above, is intimately related to information. Information, abstractly defined, is the content of a signal that conveys something about the state of the world. The signal could include the light that reflects off your skin, soundwaves coming from your mouth as you talk, or any other change in the physical world that can be sensed. Signals can carry information enabling the receiver to determine something about the state of the transmitter. The light reflecting off your face is the signal that conveys the information that you appear angry or happy or asleep.

Information flows off us constantly and we cannot control all of it. As we interact with our environment, our interactions change the state of the world. These changes create signals that can often be observed, directly or indirectly, by others. Light bounces off my face and out my window. As I walk through a room, I disturb air molecules, raise the temperature, and leave behind scents. When I touch a glass or a doorknob, I leave fingerprints. My phone, seeking to connect to wireless networks, broadcasts its approximate location. We cannot halt or fully control this information flow unless we stop interacting with reality. In fact, actions to control information flows themselves generate information. A person wearing a hoodie and a ski mask might be perceived as suspicious *because* they are interfering with light reflecting off their face. To be able to fully control information about you would require a godlike ability to control reality, including how others perceive it. If you somehow were able to eliminate the information flowing off you, you would quite literally disappear from the universe.

We learn at a very early age that there are the limits to our own control over information flows in the physical world. For example, because we cannot directly control the light that reflects off our bodies, we wear clothes, build doors, and install blinds to physically block such signals. Used this way, clothes, doors, and blinds are *perception constraints* on information: they block other people's ability to access information. Other perception constraints are physical limits on other people's ability to capture such information. For example, the slight temperature rise I might cause when walking through a room will not linger long, and once enough time has passed, people will not be able to perceive it.

Whether we're wearing clothes or closing the blinds, there are some obvious benefits to blocking what others can perceive about us. Privacy gives us space to be alone, to think, to be vulnerable, and to try new ideas. It can keep us and our belongings safer and more secure. It can maintain mystery and promote intimacy. It enables us to shape the image we present to others.

On the other hand, much of human progress has been due to scientists and innovators removing barriers to information flows so that we can better understand and connect with the world around us. Devices like microscopes and telescopes enable us to gather information from signals we couldn't previously detect. Cameras allow us to share a representation of a scene with others who are not physically present. Communications networks enable us to speak to others far beyond the distance our voices can carry. Each of these technologies expands our ability to perceive information about the world around us, including information about other people.

In part due to the many benefits of increased information, sometimes it is not possible, practical, or desirable to stop other peoples' *perception* of information about us. We want the benefits of good uses of information about us. In these cases, social norms, private rules, and law often constrain how others can *use* the information they gather in order to prevent abuses. Thus, Carol may perceive information about Bob, but social pressure, private agreements, or government regulations restrict how Carol can use that information. An example of a social norm might be people looking away when someone is entering their password or shaming people who use their camera phones in a locker room. Use constraints can vary in degree from complete bans on using certain types of information to generally allowing uses except for certain restrictions.

Perception constraints like doors or strong encryption rely on natural properties of physics or mathematics to block others from getting information about us. In contrast, use constraints stop people from misusing information about us depending on the strength of the underlying social norms or the abilities of private or government enforcers.

Every privacy policy debate is over whether and how legal use constraints should supplement the existing perception constraint and nongovernmental use constraints such as manners and norms. The debate is erupting today because, as mentioned earlier, the internet has increased the amount of information available about us. The internet has generated new categories of information about us but has also weakened or eliminated certain perception constraints. Past technologies have caused similar debate—the portable camera spurred a wave of privacy concerns in the early 1900s.[186] Those debates often resolve as individuals and society adapt to the change in legibility, including at times by adopting new perception or use constraints.

APPLYING THE FOUR TACTICS

As society adapts to changing technology that affects privacy, there are a wide number of tools available. These include shifting social norms, technological changes, private agreements, soft law, enforcement of common law or general consumer protection laws, and new legislation.[187] The four tactics laid out at the end of Chapter Seven provide one way to evaluate and compare the forms of these various tools in general or to compare specific proposals of how to use these tools.

To simplify and shorten this example application of the four tactics, I will limit myself to comparing how two different federal privacy approaches in the US measure up. Contrary to common perception, the US does have federal privacy protections. These protections take two forms. First, there is a rule-based, statutory approach. Congress has passed statutes that regulate the privacy practices of specific industries, such as

---

186 Louis Brandeis and Samuel Warren, "The Right to Privacy," *Harvard Law Review*, 4 no. 193,(1890). (arguing that common law protects a right to privacy in the wake of the popularization of the portable camera).

187 Neil Chilson, "When Considering Federal Privacy Legislation," *Pepperdine Law Review*, 47 no. 917, (2020).

financial, credit, and health. In these sectors companies must follow detailed *ex ante* rules established by Congress and/or regulators. These rules typically limit what kind of information can be collected and under what conditions, how it can be used, shared, and stored, and when it must be discarded.

For sectors without specific regulations, the Federal Trade Commission uses its consumer protection authority to bring *ex post* enforcement actions when it believes companies' use of consumer data has been unfair or deceptive. Like common law, this case-by-case enforcement doesn't impose detailed requirements on companies ahead of time but focuses on identifying and solving problems as they occur.[188]

Outside of the privacy context, lawyers, economists, and philosophers have long debated statutory versus enforcement-driven common law approaches, or what is often referred to as the rules versus standards debate.[189] There are many benefits and detriments to each. This example is not intended to rehash that entire debate. My purpose is to evaluate these two approaches to privacy under the four principles proposed in Chapter Seven.

TACTIC 1: MINIMIZE SIMPLISTIC LEGIBILITY

Case-by-case enforcement of privacy standards minimizes simplistic legibility. Even ignoring the content of the rules and standards being compared, rules by their nature impose

---

188 Daniel J. Solove and Woodrow Hartzog, "The FTC and the New Common Law of Privacy," *Columbia Law Review*, 114 no. 583, (2014): 585–86.

189 Louis Kaplow, "Rules Versus Standards: An Economic Analysis," *Duke Law Journal*, 42, (1992): 557 - 629, Cass R. Sunstein, "Problems with Rules," *California Law Review*, 83, no. 953, (1995).

more legibility than do standards. Rulemaking is characterized in part by imposing legibility on the governed practices
and entities. For example, privacy statutes, whether sector
specific like the Health Information Privacy Protection Act
or economy-wide like Europe's General Data Protection Regulation, define many characteristics of information and business practices. Is data sensitive or nonsensitive? Personally
identifiable or anonymized? What counts as "health data"?
Such statutes place regulated companies into categories such
as "data processor" or "data controller." During the legislative process, stakeholders fiercely debate such regulatory
definitions because those definitions create simplified, legally
significant categories that will apply to future types of information. Creating definitions that apply in multiple situations
requires distilling what is common across scenarios and dis-
carding the unique context of each situation. The broader the
applicability of the definition, the more total context must
be discarded to form a workable definition. That's why, for
example, it is easier to define "sensitive" or personal information in a sector-specific privacy law (like financial services)
than it is to define that same term for all sectors.

Case-by-case enforcement imposes less legibility. The FTC
brings privacy cases against companies when they violate
general principles like "unfairness" and "deception." Those
terms are not defined ahead of time. Instead, the meaning
of those concepts in the privacy context are developed over
time through application of judgment to different sets of facts.
Those concepts are further fleshed out by FTC "soft law" in
guidance and reports. Many of the same terms defined in privacy legislation are described in such guidance. For example,
the FTC discusses what is sensitive personal information in

reports, consumer and business education, and case complaints. But the FTC's descriptions are inductive and common-law like, looking back to past specific cases to provide guidance for future decision-making. For example, in any specific case the FTC may need to determine whether certain information is sensitive or not. Such categorization arguably imposes legibility on the facts of that case. But the effect of assembling a definition over dozens or hundreds of cases is more like the microscope—one of discovering what the term means rather than imposing it.

Such standards are necessarily more difficult to summarize than rules. Indeed, companies often complain that the FTC's privacy and data security requirements are not clear, for example. This is a downside of standards and, indeed, a direct consequence of avoiding simplistic categories.

TACTIC 2: TEMPER AMBITIOUS PLANS WITH PRUDENCE AND HUMILITY

Case-by-case enforcement reflects more prudence and humility than "comprehensive" privacy legislation. Case-by-case enforcement avoids high modernism better than rule-based approaches and provides more opportunity for regulatory humility. Case-by-case enforcement is incremental: the standards evolve slowly as new cases are considered. And while each case forms precedent for future cases, if the revised principle isn't a good fit in future cases, it can be modified or reversed without too much disruption.

Compare that with what is often called "comprehensive" privacy legislation. As the descriptor indicates, such plans are often broad in scope, attempting to set detailed rules for every industry and business model that exists now or will exist. Such rules are typically discontinuous rather than incremental—the laws come entirely into effect upon the entire industry on the effective date. And they are difficult to revise or reverse, with amendments taking on the same order of time as the original laws.

Of course, some legislation and rules are crafted more prudently than others. For example, all else being equal, sector-specific legislation suffers less from the knowledge problem than does comprehensive legislation intended to apply to the entire economy. Similarly, legislation that adopts general, outcome-based principles ("don't deceive consumers," for example) are more prudent and incremental than are mandates to implement specific practices ("include this specific list of disclosures in your advertising," for example). Finally, delegating rulemaking authority to an agency can minimize the need for Congress to predict future developments—although the agency then faces a similar challenge.

TACTIC 3: REDUCE THE PLANNER'S ABILITY TO IMPOSE A PLAN

Case-by-case enforcement reduces the planner's ability to impose broad privacy rules. By its very nature, case-by-case enforcement is not conducive to imposing a plan. Government enforcement addresses at most a handful of individuals or firms at a time. It typically involves a limited set of specific actions by those parties. The injunctive remedies imposed can be detailed and lengthy (FTC settlements are typically for twenty years, for example), but they usually only apply to the defendant. It may be possible to implement a complex plan involving many parties using the tools of case-by-case enforcement; a Boston federal district judge managed the desegregation of Boston public schools in the '70s and into '80s, for example.[190] But its rarity speaks to its difficulty.

One of few areas of broad agreement in the privacy debate is that the FTC's case-by-case enforcement approach limits its ability to impose across the board privacy rules. Many people argue that new privacy legislation ought to remedy this by delegating substantial and broad rulemaking authority to the FTC. Others oppose broad rulemaking authority, believing that the current case-by-case approach is preferable or arguing that Congress should establish any such detailed rules. So, while people disagree on whether it is a good thing, most everyone would agree that the current general privacy approach in the US limits the FTC's ability to impose detailed plans, satisfying Principle 3.

TACTIC 4: INCREASE THE ABILITY OF PARTICIPANTS TO RESIST PLANS OR TO SHAPE THEM

Participants can challenge case-by-case enforcement of privacy standards more easily than a comprehensive privacy law or regulations, although challenging either remains quite difficult. Enforcement actions provide each defendant with an opportunity to challenge the action in court and with due process protections. No matter the standard in place, the accused violator has a chance to persuade a neutral decision-maker that the standard is wrong or that it does not fit the facts of his situation.

---

190 Bruce Gellerman, "'It Was Like A War Zone:' Busing in Bost," *WBUR*, (September 5, 2014).

Honestly, though, neither the standards-based approach nor the rules-based approach get us very far toward Scott's recommendation that systems find ways to deeply incorporate the knowledge and values of participants. Neither approach is particularly inclusive. The participants who can share knowledge and values in a case-by-case approach are primarily the accused violators. There are many other participants in a privacy enforcement system, including the customers or users of the accused business. Their views may not be well represented in court. Even worse are rules-based approaches, which cannot incorporate all local context present at the adoption of the rules, let alone future contexts where the rules will apply.

Even represented participants face an uphill battle in fighting an enforcement action. For this reason, most defendants in FTC privacy enforcement actions settle with the Commission. Challenging a statutory or regulatory rule is, as a general matter, even more difficult, requiring a constitutional challenge or overcoming what is known as *Chevron* deference to an agency's decisions. Under this tactic, then, there is a slight preference for case-by-case approaches to privacy over rulemaking approaches.

In short, reviewing these two approaches to protecting privacy under the four principles suggests that, compared to legislative approaches, the case-by-case approach much more clearly aligns with tactic one, two, and three, and is perhaps slightly better on tactic four.

CONTENT MODERATION

One of the most contentious issues in technology policy today is how various social media companies deal with user-generated content on their platforms. Each day, users post billions of pieces of content to popular internet platforms such as Facebook, Twitter, YouTube, and Reddit. The sheer volume of user-contributed content is astounding. Twitter users post more than six thousand tweets per second. More than five hundred hours of video is uploaded to YouTube every minute.[191] More than 1.8 billion people use Facebook every day to share content and to comment on the content of others.[192] Facebook and Instagram users did fifty-five million live broadcasts on New Year's Eve 2020.[193] The much smaller Reddit community ("only" fifty-two million daily active users) still had 830,000+ posts per day and more than 5.4 million comments per day in 2020.[194]

As one might expect, when dealing with this volume of content, not all of it is truthful, friendly, uplifting, and positive. Some portion of user-generated content, small in percentage but large in absolute terms, is deceptive, mean, insulting, and bullying. And some of it is vile, despicable, pornographic, and even illegal. The platforms where users post this content have to choose how to define and handle offensive and illegal content. As one might expect when dealing with so much content, there are mistakes. Even if content moderators get

---

191 Susan Wojcicki, "YouTube at 15: My personal journey and the road ahead," YouTube, accessed February 16, 2021.

192 "Facebook Reports Third Quarter 2020 Results," Facebook, accessed February 16, 2021.

193 "Facebook's Apps Helped People Celebrate the New Year Together, Even When Apart," Facebook, accessed February 16, 2021.

194 "Reddit's 2020 Year in Review," Reddit, accessed February 16, 2021.

99.99 percent of moderation decisions correct, that's something like six mistakes every ten seconds for Twitter.

These close calls and mistakes have people of diverse political views worrying that popular internet platforms are moderating user-contributed content in a way that is harming free speech or disrupting democracy in the United States and around the world. Many, especially on the right, fear that these companies exhibit political biases in choosing what content to suppress or promote. On the left, many believe that these platforms facilitate hate and normalize extremism. Both fear that these online platforms hold outsized power over public discourse because so much speech flows through them.[195]

As a result, the platforms face conflicting social and political pressure to set policies.[196] They are being lobbied to choose policies that will benefit certain interests over others. But the content moderation debate is a great example of the problems that come from expecting centralized solutions to address emergent phenomena. So how might platforms address the concerns motivating this debate consistent with the emergent order involved?

APPLYING THE FOUR TACTICS

For the privacy example we compared two different government solutions. But the tactics can also guide private action. In the US at least, because of the protections of the First

---

195 Neil Chilson and Casey Mattox, "[The] Breakup Speech: Can Antitrust Fix the Relationship Between Platforms and Free Speech Values," *Knight First Amendment Institute*, March 5, 2020.

196 Ibid.

Amendment, the government does not do content moderation. Content moderation of these platforms is largely up to the companies themselves.

The principles remain relevant to private decisions affecting large, complex system like many social media platforms. In some ways, platforms are like governments with regard to their users. This comparison has significant limits—the most important being that these platforms lack a monopoly on legitimate force, meaning that actual governments can still impose rules on them. Still, these companies possess a high degree of control over the design of the applications and services they offer to users. Indeed, their technical ability to design the entirety of the user environment surpasses the ability of even totalitarian governments to modify the physical or social environment of their subjects.[197] Practically speaking, and in part because of the lack of a monopoly of force, platforms face many constraints that authoritarian governments would not: investor influence, user feedback, local laws, market forces, etc. Still, platforms' high level of control over their users' environments means that platforms could benefit from applying the four principles as they seek to execute scalable, ambitious plans over large populations.

TACTIC 1: MINIMIZE SIMPLISTIC LEGIBILITY
As noted above, platforms have nearly complete control over the technical functions of their platforms and their user's experience. These designed environments are already highly

---

197 Neil Chilson, "Seeing (Platforms) Like a State," forthcoming in the Catholic University Journal of Law and Technology.

legible, at least for the platforms' purposes, and so there is risk of overly-simplistic legibility.

However, there is significant context-specific, illegible information in the millions of communities that have formed on these platforms. The social norms in "The Dad Gaming" Facebook group likely differ significantly from the "Retired or thinking retirement?" group and both are likely quite different from the "Environmental Professionals" group. The people in these communities likely find very different things interesting, off-topic, insulting, or offensive. If Facebook tried to set detailed rules about proper behavior that applied to all groups, such rules could not capture much of the context specific to any single group.

Instead, Facebook and several other social media platforms allow varying degrees of moderation to occur within the community itself. Some platforms provide moderator tools for admitting and removing members. Other "moderation" is simple feedback from fellow members reinforcing or discouraging unaligned behavior, either directly to the individual users or to group administrators.

All major platforms do have baseline standards for user-contributed content, however. It is typically the platform acting on these policies that raises the policy issues mentioned above. Drawing this baseline is challenging, as interest groups lobby to shape these policies. People might lobby Facebook to ban a flat earth group rather than simply not join such a group. Or they might lobby the government to impose such policies on the platforms. The further from the community the source of the rules is, and the more generally applicable such rules are intended to be, the more context the rules will ignore, and the more simplistic the legibility imposed.

TACTIC 2: TEMPER AMBITIOUS PLANS WITH PRUDENCE AND HUMILITY

Critics of how platforms are currently doing content moderation often call for the companies to invest more money, hire more staff, and develop and deploy more sophisticated screening algorithms to deal with content problems. They call for industry-wide consortiums and coordination to ensure problematic content comes down quickly. They seek comprehensive processes for users to appeal moderation decisions. Most of all, they ask for detailed, clear content moderation policies that will provide definitive answers for every situation. Many of these proposals would require sophisticated and ambitious upfront planning. Some of them have been attempted.

Today, the large social media companies have very complex content moderation procedures and policies. But none of these were the result of one-time design and implementation. Instead, the procedures and the polices have evolved over-time, frequently through changes motivated by embarrassing mistakes. The internal policies are frequently updated as new kinds of problematic content are flagged by governments, press, third-party civil society groups, and users.[198] Facebook has even created an institutional process for appeals (see below for more detail) that will help build a body of

---

198 Kate Klonick, "The New Governors: The People, Rules, and Processes Governing Online Speech," *Harvard Law Review*, 131, no. 1598, (April, 2018).

precedential decisions to guide future moderation decisions—much like common law in a legal setting.[199]

Designing and implementing a comprehensive content moderation plan in one fell swoop is doomed to fail. Incremental, piecemeal experiments cobbled together over time are likely to be more robust and well-tested. For example, in dealing with misinformation, rather than adopting a comprehensive initial plan that attempts to cover all categories of potential misinformation, platforms could identify one narrow category of misinformation to focus on. They could test several different techniques for identifying this type of content and how to deal with it (removal, flagging, account banning). This would allow platforms to learn from user feedback and understand how misinformation producers react to new policies, and then apply those lessons to broader categories of misinformation.

TACTIC 3: REDUCE THE PLANNER'S ABILITY TO IMPOSE A PLAN

Platforms already face some constraints on their ability to impose a plan on their users. Some of these constraints include commercial pressures from consumers, dictates of local law, and investor interests.

One way to further limit a platform's ability to impose a central plan would be to strengthen any of these constraints. For example, local laws could be changed to limit platforms' abilities. Of course, such laws themselves have all the potential flaws of centralized decision-making and should be evaluated

---

199 "Oversight Board," Oversight Board, accessed March 31, 2021.

accordingly. Additionally, in the US, the First Amendment limits the extent to which the government can compel or forbid the posting of certain kinds of content.

Platforms could themselves limit their own ability to impose certain plans. They could make legally binding promises about how they will use or change the platform. They also could push decision-making out to independent organizations or standards bodies. Facebook has taken an incremental step in this direction with the creation of the Facebook Oversight Board, which is authorized to review specific user appeals of Facebook content moderation actions, such as removal of content or failure to remove content.[200]

Mike Masnick has proposed that companies limit their ability to impose plans by adopting "protocols, not platforms."[201] Protocols are the standardized online recipes for how different computers talk to each other. For example, the SMTP protocol allows a wide variety of different programs (such as Gmail and Outlook) to read and send email. Masnick describes how, over the past twenty years, companies have moved away from using open protocols and toward centralized platforms where the company controls the whole interaction. This increased control has benefits, such as the ability to improve the service more rapidly and the ability to monetize. But these benefits come with "demands for responsibility, including ever greater policing of the content hosted on these platforms," as Masnick notes.[202] By shifting back

---

200 Ibid.

201 Mike Masnick, "Protocols, Not Platforms: A Technological Approach to Free Speech," *Knight Institute*, August 21, 2019.

202 Ibid.

toward open protocols, the companies would decentralize content moderation decisions and reduce their ability to interfere.

Yet another technological approach would make certain types of control technically impossible. For example, in 2020 Mark Zuckerberg announced that Facebook would being to emphasize encrypted private chatroom functionality.[203] Facebook would not be able to see encrypted user content, let alone moderate it. Such a self-imposed reduction of legibility would limit Facebook's ability to review or moderate certain content.

TACTIC 4: INCREASE THE ABILITY OF PARTICIPANTS TO RESIST PLANS OR TO SHAPE THEM
Users of social media platforms already have a greater ability to resist platforms' content moderation plans than subjects of a totalitarian government. They can forgo using such platforms, although it might be inconvenient. Many groups have also been able to effectively organize protests against certain social media platform choices using the very social media platforms themselves.

Platforms could, however, enhance the ability of users to resist undesirable plans. They could create tools that empower various users or groups of users to help govern themselves and their communities. Such tools could include consumer review and ratings systems, deputizing users, creating more broadly accessible moderator tools, and incentivizing

---

203 Paresh Dave, "Zuckerberg says Facebook's future is going big on private chats, *Reuters*, March 6, 2019.

beneficial user behavior. Platforms like Wikipedia, Reddit, and Discord extensively use such tools and benefit from the social norms that have developed around them. These tools enable users to incorporate their knowledge and *mētis* into the platform and evolve as their group changes. Facebook has somewhat similar moderation tools available in Groups. Masnick's protocol approach would also empower users by providing them with the ability to pick and choose from a wide range of moderation tools.

Social media companies also could further embrace Tactic Four by making it easy to port their data and connections to another platform ("data portability") or to access their information on one platform from another ("interoperability"). If users can more easily leave a platform for a competitor, they can more easily resist centralized plans they dislike.

In sum, social media platforms are deeply involved in complicated schemes to control the content on their platforms. They are struggling to deal with the political pressure to act as well as the practical challenges of dealing with so much content. As these companies continue to evolve their processes, following the tactics above will help limit missteps.

CONCLUSION

Hopefully, the examples above have helped demonstrate the utility of viewing public policy problems through the lens of emergent order. This approach does not offer all the answers; indeed, it would be the antithesis of emergent order thinking to claim that there was any one solution to something as complex as policymaking in privacy or content moderation. But we can facilitate emergent order solutions to highly complex policy problems like the ones discussed above if we:

- Preserve important local context rather than forcing a centralized vision of the problem;
- Seek to progress through incremental experiments rather than by deploying grand and complex schemes;
- Search for voluntary approaches that don't require mandates;
- Empower boots on the ground stakeholders to contribute their local knowledge.

CHAPTER 9

Your Actions Still Matter: They Can Change You

———

"All great changes are preceded by chaos."

— DEEPAK CHOPRA[204]

In 2018, I went fly fishing for the first time. It was a rainy day in August near Aspen, Colorado. Fly fishing is an odd sport: you stand in chilly water, often up to your waist, waving a stick with a weighted line at the end of which is a simulated bug. You can fly fish for any kind of fish. But that Colorado day I was seeking the most common fly fishing target, trout.

Trout are one of the sharpest-eyed species of fish. They must be, to snatch their food as it passes by in fast moving streams and rivers. There is a secret to finding trout in a river, my guide told me that first day. Trout like to be close

———

204 Deepak Chopra (@DeepakChopra), "All great changes a preceded by chaos," Twitter. July 1, 2018, 8:43 AM.

to the tumbling, fast water because that current brings food. But trout also need to conserve energy. As a result, they are always looking for slow, stable water near fast water—seams, shelves, or pools.

Different kinds of trout have different preferences for where they sit in a river. My favorite are brown trout, which have a boring name but are beautiful fish, with brassy and white bodies peppered with dark spots haloed with yellows. Brown trout excel at finding a tiny pocket of stillness in the middle of tumbling waters, holding their position without seeming to exert any effort. They find the stable water in the midst of chaos.

That sounds very Zen: find the stillness within the chaos. But note that while the trout chooses the still spot, they didn't themselves create that spot. The trout chooses, but the environment shapes the trout's choices.

Like trout, our environment influences our choices. Unless we make a conscious effort, we slip into the most comfortable spot in our mental and physical environment, the one that requires the least effort while giving us access to something we value or desire or enjoy. Maybe that's making the tenth snack of the day, or watching reality TV, or doomscrolling Twitter while you're supposed to be writing a book chapter...

Where was I? Oh right, our environment affects our choices. You are, yourself, a dynamic process that adapts to feedback from your environment. This is true for your physical body and for your mind. The emergent nature of our bodies and our minds means we can change ourselves but not through command-and-control. It's probably obvious that you cannot simply command your physical body to change; you can't just tell yourself to be stronger or skinnier (I wish!). But many people think it is possible to change their thought processes by simply commanding themselves to be more focused or patient or present or self-disciplined.

They're wrong. And anyone who's ever broken a New Year's resolution knows it.

Like the trout, environment shapes our choices. Unlike trout, our choices can also affect our environment. As a young teen, I delivered the local newspaper to approximately fifty of my neighbors around our suburban block in upstate New York. Every day I would cut through one neighbor's yard by stepping on a bare space in the ground cover that bordered her sidewalk. One particularly philosophical day, I wondered if I stepped there every day because it was bare—or was it bare of ground cover because I stepped there every day?

And I suddenly realized that both are true. I shape the world and it shapes me back. Pretty heady stuff for an afternoon of slinging papers.

I've occasionally thought about that eureka moment in the years since, usually while hiking along a seemingly random deer path or taking a shortcut that hundreds of other feet have worn down. But it was only in the process of writing this book that I realized how that applies to changing ourselves.

We can change ourselves in sustainable, reinforcing ways if we make the conscious effort to create "bare spots" in our environment. If we can lay down steppingstones one at a time, heading in the direction we want to go, then we'll naturally find ourselves taking that path.

CHANGE YOUR ENVIRONMENT, CHANGE YOURSELF

Perhaps it seems obvious that one way to change yourself is to change your environment. If you want to stop eating sugar, don't visit candy stores. If you want to work out more, just, as a first step, show up at the gym.

But there are a couple of non-obvious implications. First, if we think of the term "environment" broadly to mean anything outside of our conscious decision-making process, it opens up more ways to change ourselves by changing our environment. Most importantly, we should think of habits as part of our environment—a special part of the environment that is more pliable and subject to our influence than, say, the weather or the architecture of our house.

Second, to productively change our environment we need to observe and experiment. Changing an environment can results in unpredictable effects. Put one kid in a military school and they conform; another rebels all the more. Because we are emergent systems, we struggle to accurately predict outcomes. But if we seek to be aware of the choices we make and perform small tests (how does the unruly child react to being given well-defined tasks by an authority figure?), we can gain a better sense of what outcomes may be—*before* paying for military school—and we can tailor our choices accordingly.

Third, when our environment changes significantly, such as when we lose a job, move to a new town, or have a child, all of our habits are at risk. But this is also one of the best times to review and improve habits. Such changes generate masses of new information and knock us out of our old equilibrium, and thus create the chaos that we can productively use to reach new maximums.

CHANGE YOUR HABITS, CHANGE YOURSELF

Habits are a part of our environment. Habits don't require conscious choices—that's why they are habits. When we form a habit, we move something from our conscious decision-making process into our environment. A habit formed becomes like a wall in our house: it constrains our conscious behavior. Like a wall, you can bust through a habit with enough effort, but it isn't easy. This is true for good habits and for bad habits.

Earlier I mentioned the "most comfortable spot," the default activity we fall into, like a trout slipping into that pocket of calm water. That spot is a habit. It is an attractor, to turn back to language I introduced in Chapter Three. No matter where we start, we are pulled toward that spot. But we can, over time, change that habit to something that brings us more lasting satisfaction, if we want. It is as if some trout could scoop out a new hollow in the riverbed.

There are some great books on the importance of habits and how to build or break them. I am a big fan of *The Power of Less* by Leo Babauta and *Atomic Habits* by James Clear. There is also significant academic research on habit formation and change. My goal here isn't to reiterate all of those lessons, but to point out how emergent order relates to those processes and how understanding emergent order can help with the habit-building and habit-breaking process.

In his book *Atomic Habits*, James Clear describes the "habit loop" in our brain. This four-step process of cue, craving, response, and reward is "an endless feedback loop" where "[t]he brain is continually scanning the environment, predicting what will happen next, trying out different responses, and learning from the results."[205] This habit loop occurs without our conscious mind being involved, or at least not fully involved. We can form habits without ever consciously choosing to do so—they are part of the emergent order of our brain and our psychology. For example, you probably tie the same shoe first every time or run through the same routine before bed every night. You probably didn't consciously pick which shoe to tie first or design your nightly routine. Both habits formed over time as you were repeatedly faced with the same problem and solved it again and again.

This unconscious formation, the emergent nature of habits, is what makes them so powerful and dangerous. Powerful because our brains can assemble a massive amount of data gathered through experience into a useful routine that saves time and energy. It's why, in an example from *Atomic Habits*, a paramedic can tell that that her father-in-law "looks wrong" and should go to the hospital, even though she cannot explain that what she is seeing is a change to the

---

205 James Clear, *Atomic Habits: An Easy & Proven Way to Build Good Habits & Break Bad Ones*, (Avery, 2018), 71.

distribution of blood in the vessels of his face because one of his arteries is blocked.[206]

But the emergent nature of habits also makes them dangerous. Habits are a relinquishing of conscious control over certain decisions and actions. Habits move some of our choices from control to mere influence. This often saves us time and energy, but it can lead us to feel like we are out of control of our own actions—the one area where we are most capable of exercising control. Tying the same shoe first out of habit probably doesn't matter, but maybe habitually drinking a couple of martinis to relax each night does. And even innocuous or helpful habits can be problematic if the circumstances change. Experienced American drivers don't have to think about the mechanics of driving—unless they find themselves driving a car in England, where everyone drives on the left side of the road.

Because habits are the result of an emergent process, they can be very resilient to changed conditions. Your habits have inertia. The cue-craving-response-reward sequence of a habit is an attractor, a feedback loop that will resist the efforts of your conscious mind to change it. Clear explains that some of the strongest habits are autocatalytic, meaning the reward itself help create the cue that triggers the craving.[207] You feel too sluggish to do anything but watch TV, but that makes you feel sluggish—so you keep watching TV. Habits will even resist changed external circumstances for some time. But you can reshape a habit or break it with consistent feedback from your conscious mind or from the environment.

---

206 Ibid. 82.
207 Ibid. 126.

THE IMPORTANCE OF AWARENESS

To provide the feedback needed to form or break a habit, then, you can either change your environment or change the direct feedback your mind has on the habit. Either way, though, you have to start by noticing that you have a habit and when it is taking over. As James Clear says in *Atomic Habits*, "The process of behavior change always starts with awareness. You need to be aware of your habits before you can change them."[208]

In much of this book I've emphasized what is out of your control. We can't control the economy, culture, or what other people do. But if there is one thing that you can control, it is what you choose to pay attention to. You can pay attention to what you do, even if what you do is driven by habit. This ability to focus your conscious mind on what you are doing, it turns out, is a powerful lever for changing yourself.

Because you are a complex adaptive system that demonstrates emergent properties, you are influenced by the feedback from the systems around you. You could decide to minimize the amount of conscious attention you apply to those influences, simply letting your body and mind be primarily the outcome of the emergent systems above and below you in the "hourglass." If the systems that surround you are supportive and positive, this might turn out "fine" in the sense that you might have a comfortable, prosperous, and outwardly successful life. Yet many people don't have healthy systems around them. And no matter how supportive and nurturing an environment, we can always improve.

---

208 Ibid. 89.

As a complex system, you are constantly changing, but not all change is improvement. Improvement is a change that is judged to be superior to the previous situation. Judged by whom? When we are talking about self-improvement, it is judged by you to be superior. To judge something, you must observe it and test it against something else. The path to *improving* yourself begins with consciousness and awareness of what you do and then testing changes with experiments.

Thus, improving starts with paying attention, and that means not just riding along with the emergent systems that surround you. It requires observing and judging the influences on you and, most importantly, observing and testing the things that you do as a result of those influences.

Many disciplines and wise people have emphasized the importance of awareness. Volumes have been written about the power of mindfulness: being present, in the moment, and mentally engaged with what you are doing. And there are many techniques for becoming more aware of what you are doing. For example, meditation trains you to become generally aware of your own thoughts. A common technique is to practice focusing on your breath and, when your mind wanders, simply noting, "Oh, I'm thinking," and then gently returning your attention to the breath.

Other techniques are more targeted. James Clear recommends taking an advance inventory of your habits, good and bad, by listing them out in a daily sequence. He also describes the "Point and Call" techniques pioneered in high-risk work environments, where, as you are doing something you describe it out loud.[209] Samuel Jackson's character in the movie *Long Kiss Goodnight* describes a variation of this, explaining how, in a new hotel room, he sings where he places things so he won't forget where he put them.[210] I think it's just as likely that by singing he engages his conscious mind in the choice of where to put his keys, for example, so he more deliberately chooses appropriate places for his keys or wallet.

However achieved, awareness is the first and necessary step to providing feedback to your own brain and body about what it is doing. And feedback is the only way to change your emergent behaviors.

IMPROVEMENT AS A PROCESS, NOT AN EVENT

The principles of emergent order demonstrate that self-improvement is a process, not an event. This is because *you* are a process, not a static object. When you are trying to break a habit or build a new one, the process is never complete because you are never complete. This simultaneously means we shouldn't be overconfident in our successes, but we should also forgive ourselves when we fail. Your past efforts to stop smoking aren't worthless because you lit up over the weekend. Building new patterns is hard, and we should seek "progress, not perfection," as Denzel Washington's character in *The Equalizer* puts it.[211]

---

209 Ibid. 63.

210 *The Long Kiss Goodnight*, directed by Renny Harlin, (1996, New Line Cinema).

211 *The Equalizer*, directed by Antoine Fuqua, (2014, Sony Pictures).

We often think of improving ourselves as a task or set of tasks to complete. We set New Year's resolutions with goals to achieve: lose ten pounds, get out of debt, get a new job, spend more time with family. But the underlying desires are for health, opportunity, fulfillment, and connection. We are never done satisfying such desires.

Thinking of self-improvement as a task to complete can lead to setting ambitious goals. We think we'll finally be complete if we start our own business, have sculpted abs, and have a perfect relationship with our family. And yes, dramatic personal change is possible. Leo Babauta went from being an overweight smoker, deep in debt, and stuck in a job he didn't like to a highly successful, debt-free marathon runner who writes a very popular blog called *Zen Habits*.[212] But as Babauta tells it in his book *The Power of Less*, the secret to dramatic changes over time is the accumulation of little changes, often one at a time.[213] Entrepreneur Jim Rhon echoes this idea: "Success is nothing more than a few simple disciplines, practiced every day; while failure is simply a few errors in judgment, repeated every day. It is the accumulative weight of our disciplines and our judgments that leads us to either fortune or failure."[214]

This is consistent with the idea of change as a process, not an event. As emergent systems ourselves and a part of emergent

212 Kasey Fleisher Hickey, "This is how the creator of Zen Habits changed his life," wavelength, accessed February 22, 2021.

213 Leo Babauta, *The Power of Less: The Fine Art of Limiting Yourself to the Essential*, (Hachette, 2008).

214 Jim Rohn, "15 of Jim Rohn's Most Motivational Quotes," Jim Rohn, accessed February 22, 2021.

systems, we are resistant to rapid major changes but resilient and accepting of small variations over time.

In fact, attempts to change too much at once are a major reason why many people abandon their attempts to improve. This shouldn't be surprising. Big changes bring lots of feedback from our existing systems, which resist changes to the patterns. Someone who hasn't run in years will get a lot of negative feedback from their body if they try to take up running by starting with a ten-mile jog. Moving to a ketogenic diet will be harder for those who live with family members who love pasta and bread.

If we recognize ourselves as complex systems that have emergent properties, it is easier to see that self-improvement isn't a series of goals but an effort to improving our own conscious and unconscious processes and systems. As James Clear writes, "Goals are good for setting a direction, but systems are best for making progress."[215] Seth Godin makes a similar point in his book *The Practice: Shipping Creative Work*:

> "We live in an outcome-focused culture. A plumber doesn't get credit for effort; he gets credit if the faucet stops leaking. A corporation is rarely judged on the long-term impact of how it treats its employees; it is judged on its earnings per share... Lost in this obsession with outcome is the truth that outcomes are the results of process. Good processes, repeated over time, lead to good outcomes more often than lazy processes do."[216]

---

215 James Clear, *Atomic Habits: An Easy & Proven Way to Build Good Habits & Break Bad Ones*, (Avery, 2018), 34

216 Seth Godin, *The Practice Shipping Creative Work*, (Penguin, 2020), 22.

Improving yourself is a process that never ends. You never fully succeed, but that also means you never completely fail. The opportunity is there, in every choice, to become a little bit better.

ATTEMPTS TO CONTROL CAN UNDERMINE CHANGE

Another reason people frequently fail at attempts to change is that they seek to control what they cannot rather than focusing on what they can control: their attention to their own actions. Attempts to exert self-control can work for short amounts of time, but they can actually be counterproductive. Same goes for trying to control our environment, especially when we seek to change ourselves without regard to how it will affect the patterns of those around us.

More control is not the key to improvement.

I always thought great drummers must be masters of control. They need clockwork rhythm, with beats timed perfectly; the drumstick like a metronome swinging, colliding with the drumhead over and over and over again—machinelike, precise—forming the foundation upon which the rest of a composition is constructed. To assemble this musical foundation, drummers must have perfect, conscious control of themselves and their instrument, right? And surely a better drummer is one that has more control over his actions.

Wrong, according to Dave Elitch. Dave is an established session musician, having come to prominence when he toured with The Mars Volta. He's worked with Miley Cyrus and Justin Timberlake, and on the soundtrack of the movies

Trolls and *Logan*. But he is perhaps best known as a master teacher of drumming technique, with an established Los Angeles teaching practice and an online course that is booming (pardon the pun) in popularity.[217] Dave has been teaching for twenty years and his students' testimonials read like the praise of religious converts: "Dave saved my arms and hands," "It changed everything," "I am changed from this day forward."[218]

You might think Elitch's online course would be called something like "Getting Control of the Beat" or "Sticking to the Rhythm." But no—Dave's course is titled "Getting Out of Your Own Way." He likens drumming to jumping rope: if you're thinking about it, you're going to trip.[219] The conscious part of the brain that says, "left-right-left" or "the next verse is coming up"—if that part of your brain is trying to control your movement as a drummer, you're screwed. Trying to control your body creates tension. In drumming, tension leads to inefficient movement, and that causes stiff sounds and an injured body. Instead, you want to be on autopilot, out of conscious control, drumming on a stage in front of an audience while your conscious brain is free to do anything, possibly even thinking about what you need to get from the grocery store.

In one of his videos, Elitch offers a very tangible demonstration of how getting out of your own way brings benefits. In the video he gently pinches a drumstick between the index

217 "Bio," Dave Elitch, accessed February 23, 2021.
218 "Lessons," Dave Elitch.com, accessed March 31, 2021.
219 "The Tim Ferris Show Transcripts: Dave Elitch (#348)," The Tim Ferris Show, accessed March 31, 2021.

finger and thumb of his right hand, holding it vertical near a drum. He then allows the stick to tip over onto the drumhead. Gravity pulls the stick horizontal, and the rebound off the drumhead pivots the drumstick back to its vertical position. With almost no motion from the drummer, the drumstick has not only dropped but also returned to where it started. The drum returns energy to the stick.[220]

Elitch explains that a tight drummer, a tense drummer, a drummer who is thinking about how to control the drumstick—he wastes that energy. That drummer actually fights against gravity and against the rebound, trying himself to push the stick against the drum and pull the stick back. By exerting too much control, the goal instead becomes harder to achieve. The drummer will struggle to improve until he gets out of his own way.[221]

Likewise, improving ourselves is an exercise in understanding what we can and cannot control. Sheer willpower is rarely sufficient for significant change. That's like grabbing the drumstick, pushing it against the drum and pulling it back. Even if it does work in the short run, it sucks up a lot of energy and it's difficult to maintain. Instead, you should work persistently and incrementally to turn the behaviors you desire into habits, relieving your conscious mind and getting out of your own way.

---

220 Dave Elitch (@daveelitch), "All Rebound (Slow-Mo)," Instagram Photo, March 30, 2021. ("When you relinquish the need to "control" and let things happen externally or outside of yourself, what you can accomplish is both effortless and limitless.")

221 Ibid.

CONCLUSION

Surrounded as we are by complex systems with orders that we cannot control and often cannot fully understand, it can feel like we're a piece of flotsam being tossed here and there on a river of complexity. Even when we manage to find balance, we might feel like the brown trout—limited to choosing the best option provided to us by our environment. But unlike the trout, we can shape our environment, including the unconscious habits that constrain much of our day-to-day life. If we think of improvement as a process rather than an outcome, increase our awareness of what we do, and avoid getting in our own way, we can build and break habits, we can shape our environment, and we can change ourselves.

CHAPTER 10

Your Actions Still Matter: They Can Change the World

"They criticize me for harping on the obvious ... if all the folks in the United States would do the few simple things they know they ought to do, most of our big problems would take care of themselves."

— CALVIN COOLIDGE[222]

My favorite action movie is the 1988 movie *Die Hard*. Bruce Willis plays John McClane, a normal NYC cop who visits his estranged wife's big company Christmas party and gets mired in a hostage situation when terrorists take over the building. John is a police officer, but he doesn't have any particularly special skills except a tenacious determination

---

222 David Pietrusza, *Silent Cal's Almanack: The Homespun Wit and Wisdom of Vermont's Calvin Coolidge*, (CreateSpace, 2008), 82.

to do the right thing even when everyone is against him. The people he is up against are highly organized and have detailed plans. The leader of the terrorists/thieves, Hans Gruber, berates his henchmen, "We do not alter the plan!" The police and the FBI who try to deal with the situation also have plans, and they don't appreciate McClane getting in the way, either. McClane has no detailed plan. As he says to Gruber, he is "just a fly in the ointment, Hans. A monkey in the wretch. A pain in the ass."[223]

Die Hard is my favorite action movie because of McClane's seat-of-the pants tenacity in the face of incredible odds. The movie shows a regular guy dedicated to doing the right thing (even if he isn't always sure what that is) who ends up making a big difference. I think we all want to believe that we would try to do the right thing even when the odds are against us, and that doing so could really make a difference for other people.

In the last chapter we talked about how understanding yourself as an emergent system can help you change yourself. But life is not just about self-improvement. Many of us want to look outward. Like John McClane, we want to help the people and organizations around us. We want to solve problems and make a difference.

But often we feel powerless. We feel like if only we were in charge, if we had control, we could make the difference that we want to see in the world. We think that it takes control to change things. And in a world of emergent order, where we have so little control, can we really change the world?

---

223 *Die Hard*, directed by John McTiernan, (1988, 20th Century Fox).

I want to show you that although you cannot control the world, you can influence it. And that your influence will be greater and more sustained if you stop trying to control things.

THE POWER OF EXAMPLE

On Thursday, December 11, 1955, a forty-two-year-old seamstress in Montgomery, Alabama, riding home after a long workday, declined to give up her bus seat to white passengers. She declined, not as part of a personal plan or an organized protest, but simply because she "was tired of giving in."[224]

Rosa Parks's personal decision that day changed her life and helped change the lives of countless others for the better. Her decision was a catalyst for a citywide bus boycott by African Americans that lasted more than a year. It was the catalyst for a legal challenge that was eventually nullified when similar cases forced the city to overturn the segregation ordinance that she was accused of violating. And it turned her into a powerful symbol of the ongoing fight for racial equality.

Consider how little control Rosa Parks had over the bussing situation. She didn't set the rules. She didn't have any allies—in fact, three other black people on the bus did get up and move when told to. She couldn't issue commands to the bus driver or the other passengers. Rosa Parks was arrested and taken from the bus. She also didn't control the community's reaction to her arrest (although she certainly

---

224 "Rosa Parks: Tired of Giving In," National Portrait Gallery, accessed March 31, 2021.

contributed to the protest effort). The only thing Rosa Parks did control was her choice to stand and move or to remain seated. But that choice made a real difference because it influenced people.

Rosa Parks powerfully illustrates the influence that one person can have, even when they are not in control. There are many stories throughout history that validate the lesson her experience demonstrates: Mahatma Gandhi, Alice Stokes Paul, Václav Havel. The history of nonviolent resistance is packed with individuals who stood up—or refused to stand up—and inspired others to act.

LEARNING THE RIGHT LESSON FROM EXAMPLES

When one reads about the powerful decision of individuals like Rosa Parks, it can be easy to believe that history is made only by great women and men who shape history out of sheer will, who control the way things will work, for good (as in Rosa Parks's case) or for bad (as in the case of so many tyrants and oppressors). Our human desire for narrative can drive us to see history as merely a series of stories about powerful individuals. This belief can be inspiring but also intimidating. But it is incorrect.

The "Great Man" theory of history was most expressly advanced by Scottish philosopher Thomas Carlyle in the nineteenth Century. He claimed, "The history of the world is but the biography of great men," and elaborated:

> "[T]he history of what man has accomplished in this
> world, is at bottom the History of the Great Men who

have worked here. They were the leaders of men, these great ones; the modellers, patterns, and in a wide sense creators, of whatsoever the general mass of men contrived to do or to attain; all things that we see standing accomplished in the world are properly the outer material result, the practical realization and embodiment, of Thoughts that dwelt in the Great Men sent into the world: the soul of the whole world's history, it may justly be considered, were the history of these." [225]

In its most extreme version, this view of history places control in the hands of the genius, the strong, the powerful, and the wise—unique people who somehow stand outside of the river of time, dam that river, and direct it to their own purposes. This is history not as an emergent process but as a story authored and controlled by great individuals. With this anti-egalitarian view, it probably comes as no surprise that Carlyle was himself deeply anti-Semitic, racist, and openly opposed the emancipation of slaves. [226]

Carlyle's theory of history was criticized by many of his contemporaries, perhaps most vocally by philosopher Herbert Spencer, who argued that so-called "great men" are, like the rest of us, the product of their social environment. Spencer, who was one of the earliest sociologists to apply Darwin's theory of evolution to human society, argued:

225 Thomas Carlyle, *On Heroes, Hero-Worship, and the Heroic in History*, (London, James Fraser, 1841).

226 David M. Levy and Sandra J. Peart, "The Secret History of the Dismal Science. Part I. Economics, Religion, and Race in the 19th Century," *Library of Economics and Liberty*, (January, 2001).

You must admit that the genesis of a great man depends
on the long series of complex influences which has pro-
duced the race in which he appears, and the social state
into which that race has slowly grown. ... Before he can
remake his society, his society must make him.
— HERBERT SPENCER, THE STUDY OF SOCIOLOGY

Thus, Spencer argued that "great" men were primarily products of their environment. This idea of "Social Darwinism" was later twisted by eugenicists and racists into a dark belief that Spencer wouldn't have recognized. (Spencer himself held some views on race that, while mainstream at the time, remain a dark blot on his name.) But his argument that so-called great men are affected by their surroundings reflects an emergent order view of history.

Historians today generally aim for a synthesis between these two poles when describing the past. History is not just a biography of the famous and powerful. The context of "everyday" lives has an enormous impact. There are acres of history's fabric woven from the threads of everyday lives. We can learn a lot about history by studying the journals, letters, and tools of everyday people. On the tapestry of history some vibrant threads stand out, but their path is shaped by the warp and weft of the forgotten individuals around them. Order emerges, influenced by many, even though in retrospect the story we tell focuses on the vibrant.

Looking back to evolution, it is easy to imagine that if amphibians could write their history, the first fish to take steps on land would have been lauded as a pioneer and an innovator, even though its decision to crawl up out of the muck was enabled by long series of changes to its anatomy and to the environment it lived in. Bold action by individuals is worthy of honor and praise—if no one took such actions, there would be no progress. But such actions take place in a context that shapes them. Women and men do great things, but everyone can and does contribute to the society that we live in and is a part of its change.

After all, Rosa Parks wasn't the first African American to refuse to give up a bus seat. In fact, in Montgomery alone at least four other women were arrested for refusing to give up a seat before Rosa Parks's arrest. Her refusal to move did not by itself cause the subsequent protests. As Martin Luther King, Jr., wrote in *Stride Toward Freedom,* "The cause [of the Montgomery protests] lay deep in the record of similar injustices."[227] Parks's arrest catalyzed the protests, but the conditions were produced by many others whom history does not know. Had those people not acted, the world would not have been ready for Rosa Parks's protest to leave its mark on history. None of this reduces the importance and significance of Rosa Parks's decision on the bus that day; it simply explains the context of such a decision.

YOU'RE NOT OFF THE HOOK

In one way, the Great Man theory, though incorrect, can be inspiring. Our heroes can inspire us. They seem so in control of history and they make a difference. Wouldn't it be satisfying to be a great man or woman? Inspired by our

---

227 Martin Luther King, *Stride Toward Freedom,* (Harper & Brothers, 1958).

heroes, we might dedicate our lives to becoming great by seeking control.

But it can also be stifling. If so few people are heroes, and if they are the ones who change and shape the world, that means most of us are just normal people. What difference can a normal person make? Likewise, the extreme version of emergent order would suggest that we have no agency—if I am meant to be a great person, I guess I will be.

Both mental models are wrong.

We should imitate the admirable qualities of those we look up to, but we must recognize that our heroes did not and do not control history. They, like us, act within a complicated web of society where their choices combine with the choices of millions and billions of others to shape the present and affect the future. Their apparent control of history is primarily a result of our human need to simplify this complex phenomenon into a story that we can understand and share.

Yet even though order can emerge, you are not off the hook. If you want things to change, you can't just wait for solutions to emerge. Even though emergent order explains why many things are as they are, it is not a justification. Some terrible phenomena, such as widespread racism, are the result of emergent order. One should not sit back and look at a system or institution and think, "Well, that is a result of emergent order, so I better not mess with it." In fact, such passive acceptance is no more compatible with emergence than with an active intervention. Any emergent order in society is the sum effect of multiple people saying, "I need to change things."

What is important, however, is to realize your position as an input to a complex process and a part of a greater whole, gain some humility from that, and be willing to evolve alongside the system. Rabbi Tarfon explained this idea in Pirkei Avot 2:21: "It is not your responsibility to finish the work of perfecting the world, but you are not free to desist from it either."

THE ROLE OF CHARACTER IN AN EMERGENT SOCIETY

Because your individual actions can impact the system around you, it matters what you do. So how do we choose what to do? Human action is the result of moral character and personal principles shaping our response to outside circumstances. As we discussed earlier, emergent order is the result of individual entities applying simple, local rules. A person's character is their most local rules. People's character shapes their actions, and those actions shape society. Thus, when many individuals in a society share similar character traits, those traits can have a very large impact.

One good example is how individual trustworthiness and willingness to trust are critical to well-functioning markets. In markets we frequently deal with complete strangers on very important issues. We hand over money without knowing for sure that we will get anything for it. We stop into a random town and eat lunch without many qualms. We shake hands on deals that perhaps lawyers could have been involved in, but which would have added much expense. Trusting others is an oil that lubricates trade, removing much of the friction that would occur if we had to button everything up perfectly to hedge every risk of someone turning out to be a cheat. In societies where trust is low, the gears of the market grind, gummed up by legalese and suspicion. As economist Russ Roberts explained it,

> *"Being trustworthy and honest maintains and helps extend the culture of decency beyond your own reach. You are a part of a system of norms and informal rules that is much bigger than yourself. When you behave with virtue you are helping sustain that system. [Just like how every time] someone hears you say 'Google' when you're talking about searching for something on the internet, you reinforce and spread the use of the word as more than a brand name. Every time you reward someone's trust or go the extra mile, you are encouraging others to do the same."*[228]

Up to this point I have not argued for any particular character or moral code but simply pointed out that our moral code influences the society around us by governing our actions. Many religions and moral philosophies grapple with how to react to circumstances outside of our control. Christianity, for example, emphasizes trust in God, the temporary nature of our existence on earth and the promise of an afterlife.[229] Buddhism emphasizes the interconnected nature of the world, even denying the permanent existence of any "self" or individual. Like many eastern religions it also encourages the training of one's mind through maintaining an awareness of what one is thinking, nurturing good thoughts while abandoning bad thoughts. One could write a whole book

---

228 Russ Roberts, *How Adam Smith Can Change Your Life*, (Portfolio, 2015), 196.

229 See Matthew 6:34; Philippians 4:11-13.

on how themes of emergent order are reflected in various religious traditions.

But the philosophy I've found to most practically address how we should act given emergent order is Stoicism. The term "stoic" today is often used to mean "tough" or "unfeeling" in response to pain or emotion. But the philosophy is far more than just having a thick skin. Core to the Stoic philosophy is the principle of the "Dichotomy of Control." The Stoic Epictetus, a former slave who became probably the most influential of the Stoics and whose work remains in print and influential today, described this as the division between what is in our control and what is not in our control. The Stoics argued that happiness comes from our application of reason to the impressions (our senses) in order to align our thoughts with reality. The dichotomy of control is essential to this process. By properly realizing what we can control and what we cannot, we can address our attentions and energies more effectively, they argue.

The Stoics view only one "thing" as under our control: our choices about how we will use the impressions of the world we receive. We cannot control the weather, but we can control how we think about the fact that it is raining. In fact, we can shape our own habits of thought through a process of constant self-examination and feedback. The first philosopher of the modern era, Descartes, was heavily influenced by Epictetus when he wrote:

> "The aim of our studies should be to direct the mind with a view to forming true and sound judgments about whatever comes before it ... [A person should consider]

how to increase the natural light of his reason ... in order that his intellect should show his will what decision it ought to make in each of life's contingencies."[230]

Remember the diagram from Chapter Six, with the mind at the neck of the hourglass, our brain and body emergent systems below us, and a multitude of emergent systems above us. Our influence ripples out in both directions, but our control is limited to our ability to improve our own reasoning about and reaction to these systems.

We're like an archer who notches an arrow, draws back the string, and aims. Once the archer looses the arrow, she cannot control it. The arrow's ultimate path is subject to the vagaries of the world: wind, gravity, obstacles. The archer controls how she draws and where she aims. She influences the arrow's path, but she does not control it.

It would be futile for the archer to try to control the path of the arrow by focusing on changing the wind or modifying gravity. Her largest contribution to the path of the arrow is her aim. She should focus on refining her aim rather than on trying to control the environment through which the arrow flies.

Likewise, we ought to focus where we have the strongest chance of affecting change. And where we have the strongest chance of affecting change is locally. We can monitor and give feedback to ourselves easily. We can observe our own thoughts. We can best shape future trajectory of events in our lives by focusing on our own thoughts and actions.

---

230 Rene Descartes, *Rules for the Direction of the Mind*, (OGB, 2011).

Stoics have a very useful approach for how to adjust our mind and emotions to the lack of control that exists in emergent systems. However, Stoics do not have an explicit theory of influence: how does what we do matter? And how can we choose what to do? Their answer is to treat things "according to their nature." Struggle and desire lead to suffering, so the best way to avoid suffering is to act according to your nature and eliminate desire. This can lead to a sort of deterministic passivity. Epictetus, for example, urged slaves to act according to their nature as slaves. While this may be more peaceful, a human appetite for justice and general improvement are left unserved by such an approach.

Ultimately, the Stoics failed to realize that the "nature" of many things is itself the result of an emergent process. And the actions of individuals affect that emergent process. As such, one's influence, even if small, matters! For example, the institution of slavery—although emergent—was not inevitable. Actions to change that institution can (and did) have influence, even if abolitionists could not control what happened.

CONCLUSION

Die Hard remains a popular and familiar film. You can probably quote John McClane's everyman turned hero. But life and history are not like the movies. Most regular people who do the right thing in the face of difficult circumstances are forgotten—if they were even noticed in the first place. While history might not remember you or me, that doesn't mean we're off the hook. Whether as individuals or as leaders, our actions matter. Our actions will affect the world, probably in ways we cannot predict and maybe in ways we will never perceive. We cannot control the outcomes of our actions. But we can influence others through our example and, by inspiring and empowering them to act, also influence the world.

CHAPTER 11

You Need Your Communities and Your Communities Need You

On July 15, 2014, pro golfer Chris Kennedy challenged his wife's cousin, Jeanette, to dump a bucket of ice water over her head. Jeanette's husband Anthony had ALS, a disease that progressively damages the brain and spinal cord. Chris thought that the ice bucket challenge, which had been percolating among pro golfers as a way to raise money for charitable causes, would at least make Anthony smile. It did far more than that. A mere two months later, over seventeen million ice bucket challenge videos had been shared on social media worldwide, including by Bill Gates, Jimmy Fallon, former President George Bush, and New York Yankee Derek Jeter, and more than $115 million had been raised to study the disease. Several ALS charities now run versions of the challenge every summer.[231]

---

[231] "The incredible history of the ALS bucket challenge," ALS Association, accessed April 1, 2021.

Chris Kennedy and the other early participants in the ALS Ice Bucket Challenge never imagined how fast the phenomena would spread or what a powerful effect it would have.

The key link between their individual action and the cumulative effect on the world was community. We've already discussed how understanding emergent order can help you improve yourself and improve the world, but one of the key tools to do both is by improving your communities and your other local institutions. Such communities are emergent phenomena, and understanding emergent order helps us understand why participating in them is important as well as how we can best contribute.

COMMUNITIES AS EMERGENT INSTITUTIONS

We are all part of many different communities where we have a role. What I am calling communities are a local subset of what economists and political scientists call "institutions." I talked to American political analyst Yuval Levin about institutions. He is the author of *A Time to Build: From Family and Community to Congress and the Campus, How Recommitting to Our Institutions Can Revive the American Dream*.[232] Levin is the director of Social, Cultural, and Constitutional Studies at the American Enterprise Institute. He currently holds editorial positions at three different publications simultaneously and, perhaps predictably, speaks in well-crafted paragraphs.

---

232 Yuval Levin, *A Time to Build: From Family and Community to Congress and the Campus, How Recommitting to Our Institutions Can Revive the American Dream*, (Basic Books, 2020.)

As Levin explained, "Institutions are the structure of what we do together." In other words, institutions are organizations of people intended to serve a specific purpose or function. Examples include corporations, government, churches, book clubs, fan clubs, alumni associations, and families. Two things define an institution: its purpose and the organizational structures that attempt to serve that purpose. The purpose and organizational structures tend to stay the same even as the individuals involved in the institution change. An institution's purpose can be mundane, such as the water or coffee clubs that some federal agency staff form to split the cost of beverages. The purpose can be personally meaningful, such as a support group for breast cancer survivors. And the purpose can be profound, such as houses of worship seeking to connect humans with universal truths.

The purpose of an institution rarely changes. It is the thing the attracts members. Levin offered an example that proves the rule in its breach. It turns out that Kaiser Permanente, the health insurance and health care provider, actually began its corporate life as a ship-building company. When the company offered health insurance to its employees, the offering became so popular that it eventually became the business of the company.[233]

The organizational structures that help define an institution can also vary widely in formality and permanence. Some institutions have formal rules, such as the charter for a homeowner's association. In addition, all institutions have organic collective habits and routines. This could include welcome

---

233 "Our History," Kaiser Permanente, accessed February 23, 2020.

routines for new members, a Monday morning all-staff meeting, or a tacit agreement among neighbors not to mow the lawn too early on weekend mornings. These kinds of organization structures represent the collective knowledge of the institution's members pursuing the institution's purpose over time. Levin, summarizing sociologist Mary Douglas's views, describes institutions as the collective result of the thought and work of many people over time—a kind of "preconception" that benefits the future members of that institution and, to use language from Chapter Two, an augment for our talented but ultimately limited brains.

Institutions are emergent. As Levin told me, "Institutions are not really top-down creatures. Generally speaking, our institutions take the shapes they do through gradual evolution over time." While institutions have a central purpose, it is the collective action of individuals pursuing that purpose that shapes the institution. Sometimes, Levin acknowledges, "institutions take corporate forms" that are "officially sanctioned and formed. But even then ... that is a kind of seal of approval on something that has already taken shape on its own." Institutions emerge like other forms of emergent order. There are feedback loops that align the incentives of members. Often, Levin notes, those feedback loops are about choice and failure. "For the individual, the capacity to make a choice among some options is at the core of how [institutional] evolution happens." Often, the option is to end something the institution is doing that isn't working. "The process is more about failure than success. It's like [biological] evolution—it's about stopping things that aren't working."

But the result, he argued, is that "[w]hat lasts gets a kind of veneration over time, and we come to think of it as our traditions." According to Levin, calling something a tradition is just one way of saying, "This has worked for a long time." We don't always know why it works; in fact, we often don't know. But the trial and error of individuals pursuing a purpose over time creates structures that can often stand decades or even centuries of change. As Levin argues, "The process through which that happens is strong *because* it is undirected."

As I mentioned earlier, communities are one kind of institution. There are many different kinds of communities, but the term generally connotes local collections of individuals. The "locality" can be and often is geographic, but online communities with geographically diverse members are increasingly common. Many of the points I make in this chapter would apply to larger institutions, such as state or federal governments or international charitable organizations. But as we will see, understanding emergent order suggests that there are very good reasons to focus locally to improve our lives and the lives of others.

COMMUNITIES UNDER THREAT?

There are two related implications of the emergent order nature of institutions. Institutions can be strengthened by the actions of the members of that institution. Conversely, even the strongest institutions can be weakened and ultimately destroyed, not only by outside threats, but by poor behavior from its members. Because of the emergent order nature of institutions, these virtuous or vicious cycles can happen relatively quickly.

The threat to community has long been discussed. Twenty-four years ago, Richard Cornuelle diagnosed the failure of community in the United States. Cornuelle argued that nonprofits and voluntary groups or "the independent sector" can provide social services—and historically had done so. During his career, Cornuelle helped to create nonprofits that provided housing, urban development, and educational loans. Cornuelle points back to a time when the average American actively participated in building his or her community. In the mid-1800s and early 1900s people pooled resources to ensure against health and financial risks in mutual aid societies. These private organizations were a key part of American life, Cornuelle observed, but starting early in the twentieth century, the US embarked on "a sustained and continuous transfer of responsibility in a single direction, away from society's most primary institutions—individuals, families, circles of friends, local voluntary organizations, local government—toward state government and in the end, inevitably, to federal government."[234]

Cornuelle argues that this happened because key institutions willingly gave up authority to the government. They did so because of a widespread "conviction that the impulse to build a good society in a more complex and interdependent world would have to be expressed primarily through the nation state."[235] This belief developed as people analogized nation states to the massive apparent success of corporations in the early 1900s. The prevailing wisdom was that these corporations were successful because 1) they gained near or

----

234 Richard Cornuelle, *De-Nationalizing Community*, (Philanthropy, 1996), 11.
235 Ibid. 10.

actual monopolies; 2) they centralized authority to enable a comprehensive oversight of all facts when making decisions; and 3) they used specialized professionals to scientifically manage ordinary workers. People began to believe that all services could be more efficiently provided the way that oil or steel was provided—through a single centralized professional organization.

Others have, in more modern times, warned of the collapse of other types of communities. In 2000, Robert Putman wrote *Bowling Alone: The Collapse and Revival of American Community*, bewailing the loss of American social capital. He provided data sets showing that participation in older ways of social interaction—Elk's Clubs, church attendance, and yes, bowling leagues—had been declining since the 1950s.[236]

Putnam's thesis has been criticized as focusing on older forms of social interaction without accounting for newer forms. Levin, in his book *A Time to Build*, has revised Putnam's theory without committing the same mistake Putnam did. Levin examines some of the new ways that we work and play together. He generally criticizes these replacement connections, particularly modern social media.

For example, Levin argues that online communities lack depth because they encourage shallow interactions. Unlike more traditional institutions, he claims there is no mutual dependence between social media users. You just tweet at someone and they tweet back at you; you don't rely on them

---

236 Robert Putman, *Bowling Alone: The Collapse and Revival of American Community*, (Simon & Schuster, 2001).

to achieve something, nor do they rely on you. This makes social media interactions largely cheap talk. We talk a lot online, but we rarely have a conversation. This leaves us connected but lonely, Levin argues.

According to Levin, this cheap talk is a result of the structures for interaction on these platforms. He argues that the advertising model of social media drives social media companies toward encouraging these types of brief, provocative, performative communications. Levin also criticizes the informality of the social media world—a lack of structure that levels the playing field but also removes restraint, protection, and unleashes online harassment. Yuval points to his own experiences with anti-Semitic trolls online as an example.

Levin further argues that these shallow interactions have infected other institutions. In particular, he points to the dysfunction of Congress, where members are less interested in contributing to the health of the institution and instead use the institution as a platform to highlight their own opinion and position. Rather than being molded by an institution, people increasingly use institutions as a metaphorical platform for themselves, standing atop and shouting.

I am sympathetic to Levin's argument. New technology—not only the internet, but other relatively modern innovations such as 24/7 cable news—has made it possible for us to be connected to larger communities. Given our limited capacity, connection to larger communities would seem to inherently mean those connections are shallower. And this can mean we neglect our local communities. For example, many of us spend time obsessing over national news and politics, where our role is, honestly, rather minimal. This draws us away from local news and politics, where our role can be much larger.

But there are reasonable grounds for pushback to Levin's skepticism. These new online platforms are very young compared to more traditional communities. No doubt they will benefit significantly from continued experimentations and failure and will evolve much as the other, much older institutions that Levin appears to prefer already have. Levin admits that platforms and we as society will evolve in our use of platforms and points out some encouraging trends but remains broadly pessimistic.

I have some personal experience with the power of online communities. While my wife was still pregnant with our daughter Alice (she is now almost two years old), Alice was diagnosed with a club foot, a birth defect that, thanks to the miracles of modern science, is entirely correctable. But correcting the problems requires a challenging process that spans years. As new parents we had many questions, concerns, and worries. Our doctors were great but not always available. You know who was always available? The five thousand plus people in the Facebook Clubbed Foot support group. At any time, day or night, we could hear from people we had never met but who understood what we were going through. And now that we're through the hardest part of this process, we can help other parents who need support.

This type of always-reachable special interest community wouldn't exist without social media. And it is just one of millions of examples of how people use platforms to build community. People are using platforms in unanticipated, noncommercial, hard to measure, and easy to ignore ways— like the Clubbed Foot support group.

The COVID pandemic, for all its tragedy, has also demonstrated how online tools can strengthen community. The economic havoc wrought by the pandemic and the reactions to it have created a lot of suffering across the world. Governments debate large spending packages intended to boost the limping economy. But in the background, with far less fanfare, people are using online tools to connect resources with those who need them. For example, the generally libertarian Stand Together philanthropic community raised more than $100 million dollars of direct cash assistance for needy families. Most of the small dollar contributions were prompted by a vigorous online ask. This money has been distributed in a decentralized manner through local organizations who best know the needs of their communities and has helped more than two hundred thousand families across America.[237] Even mutual aid societies have been given a boost by technology. Radical leftist website *It's Going Down* has assembled a list of more than two hundred mutual aid organizations in nearly every state dedicated to helping those in their community get through this difficult time.[238] These organizations operate online using tools such as Facebook Groups, Google Docs, Twitter, Discord, Instagram, and PayPal.

---

237 "What is #GiveTogetherNow," Give Together Now, accessed February 16, 2021.

238 "COVID-19 Mutual Aid," It's Going Down, accessed February 16, 2021.

THE RELATIONSHIP BETWEEN YOU AND YOUR COMMUNITIES

One need not fully accept Levin's critique of modern communities to agree with him that communities are a vital part of human thriving, and that there are things that we as individuals can do that will benefit ourselves and will benefit these communities as well.

WE SHAPE COMMUNITIES

Communities can act like an amplifier of individual action. Levin explains that "functional institutions link personal change and social change" because institutions "both enable that change to matter and enable other people to see it." In other words, institutions magnify the effort of the individuals who are a part of them.

The ALS Ice Bucket Challenge is perhaps an extreme example but fits this model. The calls of early participants to donate to ALS charities, paired with the viral nature of video and the rules around challenging other people to do it, created a phenomenon that magnified the initial effort. As Levin told me,

> "[S]mall scale change can make a huge difference precisely because the order is emergent. If you're able to build trust, for example, in social institutions, you can have a transformative effect because you begin to offer a model to other people of what can work and you create an attractive institution."

Sometimes we can change our communities by creating new ones. When I told my friend Jon that I was writing about communities, he told me about a community that affected his life. He said that when he was a kid, his family would regularly get together with a group of other families from the same synagogue, called a havurah. He still remembers many of the children's names, even though he has lost touch with them. The havurah socialized with each other, built friendships, and learned from each other.

I hadn't heard of a havurah before, but it turns out it was something like the Bible study groups that I attended as a child and teenager. It also turns out that the havurah movement was something of a rebellion.

In the late '60s, a group of Jewish friends in Cambridge, Massachusetts, were disillusioned with the formality and sterility of the average American synagogue. They wanted something different: a nonhierarchical group of equals, teaching each other and dispensing with unnecessary formalities. The movement, which spread worldwide in the 1970s, wasn't intended to replace synagogue. It was a separate side-gathering established by people who needed something in addition to synagogue. But ultimately, it did have a profound effect on long-established synagogue practices. As Jonathan Sarna, a professor of American Jewish history at Brandeis University, explained in a 2019 article, "The havurah movement has had a vast impact on synagogues. The informality so characteristic of havurot [the plural of 'havurah,'] percolated down within synagogues."[239] As a result, "so many synagogues have been rebuilt to remove the sense of the rabbi and the president towering above everyone else." [240]

---

239 Michael Wittner, "Learning with friends: The spirit of havurah is alive and well," *Jewish Journal*, January 24, 2019.
240 Ibid.

Thus, a community formed outside of a long-standing institution that wasn't meeting people's needs ultimately ended up transforming that same centuries-old institution. Without even intending to, the participants in the havurah movement shaped their community—and changed the world.

COMMUNITIES SHAPE US

But our communities are not simply conduits for our effect on the rest of the world. The communities we choose also change us. This is hardly a novel observation. We talked earlier about the importance of environment on our own behavior, and communities are a key part of our environment. Folk wisdom counsels choosing your friends carefully. Motivational speaker Jim Rohn has argued that we're the average of the five people we spend the most time with.

Beneath such proverbs lie a deeper truth. It isn't just our friendships with others that shape us. As Levin told me, "We are so inclined to see ourselves as individuals. And we too often fail to see how our individuality is formed by our relationships of obligation with other people." Those relationships of obligation, our responsibilities to others, happen within communities and other institutions. Our commitments to others—big or small—shape what we do. When I pledge to pick the next book for my book club, it means I'm going to spend a few hours looking for the perfect book, even though I might want to spend those specific hours differently when they arrive. If you become treasurer of your condo board, there will probably be some hours you wish you hadn't taken on that responsibility, but you do it anyways—out of commitment or guilt or pride, or some mix of all of the above.

There is one specific way in which communities shape us which I find intriguing. People who join together with others to solve a particular problem build collective problem-solving skills. A neighborhood that organizes to clean up a vacant lot builds relationships and communications networks that will help its members more easily address the next shared problem. And the more skilled people become at solving problems in a cooperative way, the less likely they are to seek noncooperative, often government-implemented solutions to solve their problems. Conversely, it should come as no surprise that people who are out of practice working together to solve problems will more often turn to an authority to solve the problem.

Whatever the reasons we have for taking on obligations, the promises that we make to others in our communities shape what we do. And, as we saw in Chapter Nine, what we do shapes us—because we are complex, emergent systems.

VIRTUOUS AND VICIOUS COMMUNITY FEEDBACK LOOPS

Because participants shape communities and communities shape participants, there can be virtuous and vicious cycles. A community that positively affects the lives of those who participate in it attracts loyalty and trust in that community, and that attracts others who have similar needs. The success of the Ice Bucket Challenge and the havurah movement are great examples of such virtuous cycles.

By the same token, diminished quality participation in an institution can create a vicious cycle of declining quality and declining participation. A weakening institution fails to shape its members, fails to achieve its purpose, and therefore loses trust and support. This further weakens the institution and, in some cases, only draws participants who want to use the institution for their own purposes rather than to serve the institution's purpose. Congress is a particularly prominent example of this.

But I should note that in many cases, an institution failing is perfectly fine. Institutions can outlive their usefulness, and people having the freedom to join or leave an institution serves as a kind of market signal. This is particularly true when there are many different institutions to choose from. One of the reasons government institutions are often less vibrant is because they often face little competition and thus little pressure to improve. After all, we can't opt out of Congress no matter how vicious the feedback loop becomes.

CHOOSE POLYCENTRICITY, NOT CENTRAL POLICY

Another important feature of communities is that we participate in many different, overlapping communities at the same time. Nobel prize-winning economist Elinor Ostrom and her prominent social scientist husband Vincent called these overlapping sets of commitments "polycentricity." They observed, through rigorous field study, how groups of people around the world faced and solved difficult problems through these overlapping communities rather than through top-down bureaucracies.

Elinor Ostrom's field work was vital in demonstrating that normal people are more complicated and perceptive than economic models had represented. For example, the "tragedy of the commons" is an often-cited example of market failure where a shared resource, such as a forest or fish populations, is overconsumed because every user has an incentive to take as much as they can get before it is gone. In reality, what Ostrom found was that communities around the world had sophisticated, nongovernmental governance structures to prevent overconsumption. Often, these local communities used voluntary, cooperative institutions to govern the use of commons, where economic theorists presumed only coercive governmental intervention could work. In short, Ostrom demonstrated that communities can evolve collaborative solutions to difficult economic problems without the need for centralized design and control.

Polycentricity works. But it takes close examination, like the research that Ostrom did, to identify its existence and function. As a result, when a problem is identified, polycentric approaches aren't considered. Communities are left out of the solution; instead, people turn to city, state, or federal policies to address the problem they face. It is easier, in the short run, to turn to a distant authority rather than to roll up our sleeves and work something out with our neighbors. But this short-run thinking can weaken and even destroy communities. As economist Steve Horwitz summarized, the Ostroms' "great fear, and it is a real one, was that if we did not take responsibility for governance in all of these decentralized and informal ways, we would be increasingly subject to rule from the top."[241] And once a distant official is in charge of solving a problem, people start to view the community as unnecessary. "Solve" enough problems this top-down way

241 Steve Horwitz, "10 Tips to Facilitate Collective Action From Elinor and Vincent Ostrom," Libertarianism.org, accessed February 22, 2021.

and there will be no reason for people to engage with their communities. Polycentricity will break down if we let it.

CONCLUSION

Communities can form around any common purpose, whether it be a shared geographic proximity or a childhood health challenge or dumping ice water over one's head for charity. We should look for chances to strengthen the many communities in which we participate. Strengthening our communities shapes us. Communities magnify our actions, helping to change the world, in part by shaping others who come along after us. By collaborating with others, we build skills in cooperation. And when we collaborate to solve local problems, we reduce the need for top-down, distant solutions to local problems.

As we participate in our communities, we should keep emergent order in mind. Local communities are going to have the biggest impact on you, and you can have the biggest impact on them. This doesn't necessarily mean geographically local, but local to your interests and abilities. Choose communities that you can help improve and that will help shape you to become the person you hope to be.

CHAPTER 12

Six Principles of the Emergent Mindset

Whether we are seeking to change ourselves, our world, or our communities, there are key principles that can be distilled from the lessons we've explored in this book. These six principles together form the "emergent mindset." This is a mindset sensitive to the dynamic nature of the world, cognizant of our limited control, respectful of the emergent nature of our own minds and bodies, and serious about the importance of the choices we make.

Principle 1: Expect complicated results even from simple actions. We learned in Chapter Three that complex group behaviors can and often do emerge from many interactions of individual actors following simple rules. In nature, we see complexity emerge in ant colonies and flocking birds and firing neurons. In human society we see it in the "wave" at sporting event but also in language and markets and the development of cities and so many other areas of human endeavor. When we take a seemingly simple action, we might expect a predictable result, but when that action feeds into a complex system, we should expect the unexpected. Similarly, when we see a complex phenomenon, it might be generated by some relatively simple individual behaviors, repeated many times across many individuals.

Principle 2: Don't try to control what you cannot. Your actions contribute to many larger systems, but usually it's impossible to draw a straight line from what you do to the outcomes. All but the simplest events have multiple, inextricably integrated causes. Most importantly, what other people choose to do isn't your fault—and it isn't to your credit, either. You cannot control what others do, but you can choose how you react. In fact, the only thing you have substantial control over are your actions. Focus there.

Trying to control things you ultimately cannot control is a recipe for stress in personal life and a prescription for disaster in public policy. Attempting to exert control isn't just futile; it can actually destroy the very thing you are trying to preserve—like grasping an eddy in a stream. Leaders can issue commands, but skilled leaders will think of those commands as signals that are inputs to other complex processes—including people. That signal can have a great deal of influence, but it might not achieve what you want. And "what you want" may turn out to have unintended consequences. Growing frustrated when the results from a command differ from what you desired might be a natural impulse, but it is rarely useful.

Principle 3: Be humble. If you cannot control the outcomes of your actions, you should be modest in your promises to others and yourself. Don't fall for what General McChrystal calls "The Attribution Myth." Your successful leadership depends heavily on others, and your efforts might not work. The broader the potential effect of your actions as a leader, the more humble you ought to be about the potential effect and the likely outcome and the more counsel you should seek from those affected. The closer the effect to your own areas of personal experience and knowledge, the more predictable the effect. But as one moves the center of action from yourself to your family to your community to your government, the harder it becomes to predict outcomes of even what seem like simple changes.

Principle 4: Push decisions down close to the important information. Emergent systems work best when there are simple rules at the lowest level at which the relevant information exists. Rules can be simpler at the local level because the domain is smaller and there is less of a need to relay reliable information. Rather than centralizing decision-making several levels removed from the facts, empower those emergent systems whose boundaries contain the most relevant facts and where the effects will be most directly felt.

We have seen many examples of this principle throughout the book. In Chapter Five, we discussed the benefits of leading by inspiring and empowering others, rather than commanding them. In Chapter Seven we explored the difficulties of moderating content through one-size-fits-all, top-down approaches. And we saw in the Chapter Eleven the power of acting in one's local community, including the benefits for the community and for ourselves.

Principle 5: You can make the world better by making yourself better. You are part of many different dynamic, complex adaptive systems. You have influence, even though you do not have control. But by taking control of what you can—yourself—and no longer grasping for the rest, you can help the various systems which you participate in to become more fitted to their function. We saw in Chapter Ten the power of good examples like Rosa Parks. The lesson is that other people see how we act. Our acts can inspire or disgust others. And our example is a major avenue for us to influence others and thereby impact the world.

Principle 6: Learn from constraints—and choose them well. Constraints such as habits or routines are the simple rules that often enable emergent order to produce something complex in our lives or our society. Routines and habits are the result of feedback loops. When you exercise conscious decision-making repeatedly, for example, you push the complex system that is your body and mind toward a new pattern that can maintain its shape in the face of varying conditions. Recognize the wisdom accumulated in habits and routines. But don't be a slave to them. Be open to revision because conditions will change. Periodically review your habits to see if your unconscious choices are still serving your conscious needs.

Societal institutions, too, are the result of untold individual choices. We can think of them as the habits, routines, and processes of groups. When we participate in an institution, like a church or a social norm, we help shape and perpetuate it. And the institution also shapes us. Just as we should pick our habits carefully and work to develop them, we should also pick our institutions carefully and consciously and seek to strengthen them as well.

***

As I noted in the introduction, these principles are not easy to practice to their fullest. They require us to embrace our own autonomy and to act to change the world while simultaneously admitting the limitations that come from being a part of something much bigger than ourselves. But, in true emergent fashion, we do not need to practice them perfectly in order to help shape our own lives and the lives of those around us.

If understood, even if practiced imperfectly, these principles offer a real chance to productively grapple with the increased complexity of the world and of our lives. They will help us recognize the emergent order that results when we get out of control.

Conclusion

———

In 2018, I stood on stage in front of a large auditorium at a Federal Trade Commission event full of serious technology policy lawyers, economists, advocates, and engineers and told them that the most thoughtful and insightful policy movie ever made was Warner Bros' 2014 film *The Lego Movie*.[242] (Mild spoilers ahead.)

In this animated film, little, yellow-faced Lego people live in a world of Lego bricks. The main villain is President Business. He is a total dictator with comprehensive designs for Legoland. He generates plans to solve every social need, using a bunch of Lego engineers trapped in a cylindrical prison. (In an inside-the-Beltway joke surely missed by the average child Lego enthusiast, he calls this prison his "think tank.") President Business believes his expert designs are superior to the weird, inexpert, or even useless designs of others. He can't understand why people might prefer different, probably inferior designs. And he imposes his designs on others,

---

242 *The Lego Movie*, directed by Phil Lord and Chris Miller, (Warner Bros. Pictures, 2014).

through soft propaganda-like ad campaigns ("Everything is Awesome" is the constant, viral musical refrain) but also through forced construction or demolition.

But there is team of rebels and a boring everyman named Emmet. Some of these Lego rebels are master builders, skilled at real-time use of the materials around them to solve the specific problem they face. Emmet isn't an expert. In fact, his allies ridicule his constructions. Yet even Emmet's absurd constructions (like a double-decker couch) help solve the problem at hand (hiding from the bad guys). Unlike President Business, Emmet and his more experienced fellow master builders don't have plans for everyone else. They apply local knowledge and their own creativity to solve the problems they face.

Obviously, President Business doesn't like the rebels. Even more so than normal Legoland residents, these rebels mess up his plans by building ugly and weird stuff. Tired of people disrupting his designs, President Business plans to superglue all his superior Lego designs into place so that no one can muck up his planned society. A fight ensues and the rebels win, in part by convincing everyday Legoland residents that it's okay for them to design and build their own solutions without a central plan.

When I talked about Legos to the FTC audience in 2018, I had no plan to write a book at all, let alone this book. But in retrospect, that movie inspired this book. *The Lego Movie* is about emergent leadership—and it quite entertainingly captures many of the lessons of this book.

President Business is a leader who goes to extremes seeking control. He is the opposite of humble; he believes his plans are the best for everyone. Rather than regulatory humility, he typifies high modernism, to return to a phrase from anthropologist James C. Scott that I introduced in Chapter Seven. He sees society as something to literally be taken apart block by block and reassembled according to his top-down plans. He embraces what can be a very strong temptation for those in power: the desire to design a single perfect policy solution. In my experience, this mindset is particularly common among those who come to policy from engineering backgrounds. After all, shouldn't it be possible to write legal code like we write computer code, to handle all the conditions and exceptions? Shouldn't a political machine work like a washing machine: just pick the proper policy cycle, turn it on, and out comes Downy-fresh law?

But as we've talked about throughout this book, humans are not bits, gears, or billiard balls. As individual humans (or Lego people) interact, the result is the dynamic, unpredictable, emergent system we call society. It's not chaos; patterns abound. Personal habits and routines, social and ethical norms, markets, institutions, political structures, and legal strictures—these are all patterns in our emergent society. These emergent patterns are not like a perfectly predictable pendulum; they are more like an eddy or whirlpool in a stream. They are recognizable and powerful but difficult to predict or control.

When President Business cannot control the individuals in Legoland, he seeks to glue everything in place according to his plans. He hates the messiness of bottom-up innovation;

he'd rather everything be under control. But, as we've seen throughout this book, imposing top-down solutions on emergent systems is often as disruptive and ineffective as plunging one's hand into a stream to grasp a whirlpool. If such solutions work at all, they do so by changing this dynamic, fluid system into a static, solid system. They freeze the stream or dam it. (Remember the Romanian steel towns stuck with 100 percent unemployment?) Like President Business's superglue, this solution is far worse than the problem.

Unlike President Business, Emmet and his friends exhibit emergent leadership. They use the materials around them to solve the problems they face. They are (or learn to be) tolerant of different approaches to solving a problem, including imperfect and "weird" solutions. Most importantly, they equip those around them with the tools, training, character, and community needed to tackle big problems in a bottom-up manner.

My goal on that stage in 2018 was to convince the audience to resist expert-designed top-down policy solutions. Don't try to be President Business, I was saying. Be like Emmett! Search for policy approaches that support emergent experimentation and that free individuals, including nonexperts, to make the most of their unique knowledge and creativity. Many problems can be solved through social, market, or technological innovation rather than legal innovation. And rather than one single comprehensive solution to a problem, there may be many partial, personal, and imperfect solutions evolving over time. We should try to capture the wisdom, experience, and the talents of the many, not just a few experts.

I'm not sure my speech succeeded. Feedback was sparse, honestly. The one piece I recall was a tweet from someone saying that her big takeaway from the FTC event was that she needs to rewatch *The Lego Movie*. Soon after, I realized that my audience was people seeking policy and legal solutions, and I was telling them that many problems don't need policy solutions. That's a hard sell. People who do policy naturally look for policy solutions. Bottom-up, non-policy solutions can feel unsatisfying to people who want a big solution to big problems.

Hopefully, I've succeeded a bit more with this book in demonstrating that bottom-up, emergent order solutions can solve big problems. If you work in public policy, I hope I've given you a new perspective for approaching policy questions. If you don't spend your days trying to solve policy problems, I hope I've offered a perspective on leadership of yourself and in your community that you can use to improve your life and the lives of those around you.

Writing this book has certainly improved my life, while also complicating it.

I quickly learned that writing a book is, itself, an emergent process. I suppose this shouldn't have surprised me, but it did. Every detailed plan I made about how the book would be developed was quickly mangled by reality. I would spend hours researching and writing a portion of the book only to replace it with a much better source I accidentally came across later when I was writing another part of the book. The structure evolved in response to feedback from editors and friends and from myself, when some time away from the document had given me a new perspective.

There were two portions of this book that most punished me—and thus taught me the most. First, coming into the book I thought I knew what emergent order was and thought I'd be able to explain it in layman's terms rather easily. Hah! Looking back, I laugh at how naïve that was. Chapter Three, where I attempt to define emergent order, went through countless painful drafts and reorganizations. If that chapter were an animal species, I forced millennia of mutation and selection on it in the last year and I'm still unsure if it will survive in the wild.

The second trying part of the book was Chapter Nine, the chapter on what emergent order means for self-development. I started this book right when the COVID-19 pandemic struck. The already complex world grew so complicated, so quickly. All my honed habits were thrown into disarray. Like many others, my wife and I quarantined at home with our infant daughter, forcing us to develop new working patterns. A year and many evolutionary dead ends later, those patterns continue to evolve. We've been separated from friends and family and community. I've missed opportunities and deadlines and let people down. Things have been better than I have any right to expect, but I've frequently stumbled in my own attempts to build new habits in this environment.

And yet, in the midst of all that personal chaos, I was writing advice to other people about how to manage their personal habits and contribute to their community. I often felt like such a hypocrite. Sometimes I still do.

I realize now that feeling is me trying to be in control.

Naval Ravikant, entrepreneur and philosopher, has said, "To write a great book, you must first become the book."[243] I now know what he means. The only way I got through Chapter Nine was to embrace my own observation that we are each a process, always changing and perpetually incomplete. The personal chaos and disorder and change of the past year is the dynamic environment from which the order in this book has emerged. A different and better me has emerged with it. This book is me passing along my observations of that process. Those observations are static and trapped in ink or bits. What I've written does not—and cannot—fully convey the underlying complexity.

Intellectually, I know that's okay. Emotionally, I'm still learning to get out of control.

We cannot superglue the world into perfection and we shouldn't try. We build what we can and then we take it apart and build again, incorporating what we've learned in the process. We draft and redraft our lives, and even when we "publish," we're not done because we're influencing the people and communities around us, and their feedback will influence us.

I am finished writing this book. You're finished reading it. But this book isn't finished. Nor am I. Nor are you. Because nothing ever is.

---

243 Naval Ravikant (@Naval), "To write a great book, you must first become the book," Twitter, May 15, 2018, 2:42PM.

Acknowledgements

———

A book is a static snapshot of an evolving web of ideas. Like all outcomes of a complex systems, its causes are deeply intertwined. But some causes stand out.

In January of 2020, Garrett Jones asked me what book I was going to write. Eric Koester's Creator Institute turned that surprising question into a project. Eric and the team at the Creator Institute and their partners at New Degree Press kept me moving on that project. Special thanks to my editors, Cassandra Casswell and Rebecca Bruckenstein, who guided me every step of the way.

The ideas in this book were generated in conversations with many people. Among them are Rob Axtell, Marisa Alford, Michael Alford, Peter Boettke, Per Bylund, John Chisholm, Carl Gillett, Jeff Jarvis, David Johnson, Yuval Levin, Jay Lloyd, Russ Roberts, Jon Schulman, and Godmund Schick. Many of these people appear in the pages of this book, several of them offered direct and helpful feedback on my written work, but all of them have shaped my thinking.

I want to especially thank Maureen Ohlhausen for giving me amazing career opportunities while also serving as an outstanding example of emergent leadership.

So many of my colleagues at Stand Together and the Charles Koch Institute supported me in this work: Jesse Blumenthal, Charlie Tapp, Andy Gillett, Parker Kobayashi, Rob Raffety, Ashley May, Jim Fellinger, and Andrew Isenhour.

My deep thanks to the participants in the Institute for Humane Studies' workshop on my manuscript: Michael Broderick and Michael Tolhurst of IHS, as well Arthur Diamond, Erin Dolgoy, Lauren Hall, Peter Jaworski, John Samples, and Adam Thierer. Thanks also to the other staff of IHS for organizing the workshop: Stewart Robertson, Adrienne DePrisco, and Emily Birchmier. And thank you to the Templeton Foundation for supporting the workshop.

Several family members helped us get through this pandemic year relatively smoothly and gave us places to retreat from DC when it was unclear how we were going to balance our new baby and work. Thank you, Michael and Shannon Alford and David and Esther Chilson for your hospitality and generosity.

I didn't get to see my parents much this year, but from them I've learned the importance of continually striving to do right, be humble, and love others—even though I fall short. I miss you.

Finally, all my love to my wife, Marisa, a profound parcel of channeled complexity, and to my favorite little bit of emergent order, my daughter, Alice.

Bibliography

INTRODUCTION

- Brooks, Aaron. "40+ Best Time Management and Productivity Apps of 2020." *Venture Harbour,* August 12, 2020. https://www.ventureharbour.com/best-productivity-apps/.

- Canaparo, GianCarlo and Zack Smith. "Count the Crimes on the Law Books. Then Cut Them." *Commentary: Criminal Justice* (blog), *Heritage Foundation,* June 24, 2020. https://www.heritage.org/crime-and-justice/commentary/count-the-crimes-the-federal-law-books-then-cut-them.

- Chilson, Neil. "On 'Beautiful Patterns' and my path toward liberty," *Neil Chilson* (blog), January 21, 2020. https://www.neilchilson.com/2020/01/21/on-beautiful-patterns-and-my-path-toward-liberty/.

- Dunbar, R.I.M. "Neocortex size as a constraint on group size in primates." *Journal of Human Evolution* 22, no. 6 (June 1992): 469 – 493. https://doi.org/10.1016/0047-2484(92)90081-J.

- Gleick, James. *Chaos: Making a New Science*. New York: Penguin Publishing Group, 1988.

- Hofstadter, Douglas. *Metamagical Themas: Questing for the Essence of Mind and Pattern*. New York: Basic Book, 1996.

- LaRosa, John. "What's Next for the $9.9 Billion Personal Development Industry," *Market Research* (blog). January 17, 2018. https://blog.marketresearch.com/whats-next-for-the-9-9-billion-personal-development-industry.

CHAPTER 1: THE WORLD IS OUT OF CONTROL

- Bercovici, Jeff. "Sorry, Craig: Study Finds Craigslist Took $5 Billion from Newspapers," *Forbes*, August 14, 2013. https://www.forbes.com/sites/jeffbercovici/2013/08/14/sorry-craig-study-finds-craigslist-cost-newspapers-5-billion/

- Boehm, Eric. "Paul Krugman Thinks You'll Be Happier with Fewer Choices. Nonsense." *Reason*, March 2, 2021. https://reason.com/2021/03/02/paul-krugman-thinks-youll-be-happier-with-fewer-choices-nonsense/.

- Chilson, Neil and Casey Mattox. "[The] Breakup Speech: Can Antitrust Fix the Relationship Between Platforms and Free Speech Values?" *Knight Institute*, March 5, 2020. https://knightcolumbia.org/content/the-breakup-speech-can-antitrust-fix-the-relationship-between-platforms-and-free-speech-values.

- *The Declining Price of Advertising.* Progressive Policy Institute. July 8, 2019. https://progressivepolicy.org/issues/regulatory-reform/the-declining-price-of-advertising-policy-implications-2/

- Evans, Benedict. "News by the ton: 75 years of US advertising," *Benedict Evans* (blog), June 15, 2020. https://www.ben-evans.com/benedictevans/2020/6/14/75-years-of-us-advertising.

- Food Industry Association. "From 1950 to 2010: How the Grocery Industry Has Changed." Accessed February 10, 2021. https://www.fmi.org/blog/view/fmi-blog/2018/05/29/from-1950-to-2010-how-the-grocery-industry-has-changed.

- Green, Penelope. "An Expert on Choice Chooses." *New York Times,* March 17, 2010. https://www.nytimes.com/2010/03/18/garden/18choice.html.

- Grieco, Elizabeth. "U.S. newspapers have shed half of their newsroom employees since 2008." *FacTank* (blog). *Pew Research Center,* April 20, 2020. https://www.pewresearch.org/fact-tank/2020/04/20/u-s-newsroom-employment-has-dropped-by-a-quarter-since-2008/.

- Hale, James. "More Than 500 Hours of Content Are Now Being Uploaded To YouTube Every Minute." Tubefilter, May 7, 2019. https://www.tubefilter.com/2019/05/07/number-hours-video-uploaded-to-youtube-per-minute/.

- Hlavaty, Craig. "When Boris Yeltsin went grocery shopping in Clear Lake." New Haven Register, September 13,

2017. https://www.nhregister.com/neighborhood/bayarea/
news/article/When-Boris-Yeltsin-went-grocery-shopping-
in-Clear-5759129.php.

- Harford, Tim. "Given the choice, how much choice would
  you like?" *Financial Times*, November 13, 2009. https://www.
  ft.com/content/9cebd444-cd9c-11de-8162-00144feabdc0.

- Kobliski, Kathy J. "Classified Ads." *Entrepreneur*, January
  17, 2006. https://www.entrepreneur.com/article/83084

- Kubu, Cynthia and Andre Machado. "The Science Is
  Clear: Why Multitasking Doesn't Work." Cleveland
  Clinic, June 1, 2017.

- Miller, Andrew. *On Not Being Someone Else: Tales of Our
  Unled Lives*. Harvard University Press, June 9, 2020.

- Miller, Ron. "The 80s were big for TV." *Washington Post*,
  December 24, 1989.

- NCTA — The Internet & Television Association. "Cable's
  Story." Accessed February 10, 2021. https://www.ncta.
  com/cables-story.

- Norberg, Johan. "Globalization's Great Triumph: The
  Death of Extreme Poverty." *Human Progress,* October
  15, 2018.

- Panday, Jyoti. "Exploring the problems of content moderation on social media." *Internet Governance Project*,
  December 23, 2020. https://www.internetgovernance.

org/2020/12/23/exploring-the-problems-of-content-moderation-on-social-media/.

- Ravenscraft, Eric. "How to Make Your Phone Limit Your Screen Time For You." *New York Times*, April 1, 2019. https://www.nytimes.com/2019/04/01/smarter-living/how-to-make-your-phone-limit-your-screen-time-for-you.html.

- Ridley, Matt. "Ridley: We've Just Had the Best Decade in Human History." *Human Progress*, January 8, 2020. https://www.humanprogress.org/weve-just-had-the-best-decade-in-human-history-seriously/.

- Rothman, Joshua. "What If You Could Do It All Over?" *New Yorker*, December 14, 2020.

- Schwartz, Barry. "Is the famous 'paradox of choice' a myth?" *PBS Newshour*. January 29, 2014. https://www.pbs.org/newshour/economy/is-the-famous-paradox-of-choice.

- Seagate. "Seagate: Our Story." Accessed February 10, 2020. https://www.seagate.com/our-story/.

- Shearer, Elisa. "Social media outpaces print newspapers in the U.S. as a news source." *Pew Research Center*, December 10, 2018.

- Shlain, Tiffany. *24/6: The Power of Unplugging One Day a Week*. New York: Simon & Schuster, September 24, 2019.

- Shopify. "Empowering independent business owners everywhere." Accessed February 22, 2021. https://www.shopify.com/.

- Vogels, Emily. "Partisans in the U.S. increasingly divided on whether offensive content online is taken seriously enough." *Pew Research Center*, October 8, 2020. https://www.pewresearch.org/fact-tank/2020/10/08/partisans-in-the-u-s-increasingly-divided-on-whether-offensive-content-online-is-taken-seriously-enough/

CHAPTER 2: OUR BRAINS, PROSPERITY, AND EMERGENT ORDER

- AI Impacts. "Transmitting fibers in the brain: Total length and distribution of lengths." Accessed February 10, 2021. https://aiimpacts.org/transmitting-fibers-in-the-brain-total-length-and-distribution-of-lengths/.

- Barker, Graeme. *The Agricultural Revolution in Prehistory: Why did Foragers become Farmers?* Oxford University Press, 2005.

- Benson, Buster. "Cognitive bias cheat sheet: Because thinking is hard." *Better Humans* (blog). September 1, 2016. https://betterhumans.pub/cognitive-bias-cheat-sheet-55a472476b18?gi=9908521466b9.

- Corkery, Michael and Sapna Maheshwari, "Is There Really a Toilet Paper Shortage?" *The New York Times*, March 13, 2020. https://www.nytimes.com/2020/03/13/business/toilet-paper-shortage.html.

- DeWeerdt, Sarah. "How to map the brain." *Nature Outlook: The brain*, July 24, 2019. https://www.nature.com/articles/d41586-019-02208-0.

- Georgia Pacific. "Statement on Georgia-Pacific's Response to COVID-19." Accessed February 10, 2021. https://www.gp.com/news/2020/10/statement-on-georgia-pacifics-response-to-covid-19.

- Ghose, Tia. "The Human Brain's Memory Could Store the Entire Internet." *LiveScience*, February 18, 2016. https://www.livescience.com/53751-brain-could-store-internet.html.

- Harrison, K. David and E. Raimy, "Language As An Emergent System." *Soundings*, 90 no. 1/2, (2007).

- Hayek, Friedrich. *The Fatal Conceit*. Chicago: University of Chicago Press, 1988.

- Luo, Liqun. "Why Is the Human Brain So Efficient?" *Nautilus*, April 2018. https://nautil.us/issue/59/connections/why-is-the-human-brain-so-efficient.

- McCloskey, Deirdre Nansen. *Bourgeois Equality: How Ideas, Not Capital or Institutions, Enriched the World*. Chicago: University of Chicago Press, 2016.

- MR University. "The Hockey Stick of Human Prosperity." March 13, 2019. Video, 4:54. https://www.youtube.com/watch?v=t9FSnvtcEbg.

- National Center for Biotechnology Information. "How does the brain work?" Accessed February 10, 2021. https://www.ncbi.nlm.nih.gov/books/NBK279302/.

- Palmer, Annie. "Why ordering from Amazon has been so unpredictable during the coronavirus crisis." *CNBC*, May 9, 2020. https://www.cnbc.com/2020/05/09/amazon-and-sellers-negotiate-delays-demand-shifts-during-coronavirus.html.

- Reed, Leonard. "I, Pencil." Foundation for Economic Innovation. Accessed April 9, 2021. https://fee.org/resources/i-pencil/.

- Ro, Christine. "Dunbar's number: Why we can only maintain 150 relationships." *BBC Future*, October 9, 2019. https://www.bbc.com/future/article/20191001-dunbars-number-why-we-can-only-maintain-150-relationships.

- Stanford Encyclopedia of Philosophy, "Self-Consciousness." Accessed March 30, 2021. https://plato.stanford.edu/entries/self-consciousness/.

- Tupy, Marian. "The Great Miracle of Industrialization." *Human Progress*, May 6, 2019. https://www.humanprogress.org/the-miracle-of-industrialization/.

CHAPTER 3: WHAT IS EMERGENT ORDER?

- Buchanan, James M. "Law and the Invisible Hand." Reprinted in *Vol. 17: Moral Science and Moral Order*. Indianapolis, IL: Liberty Fund, Inc., 2001.

- Gefland, Michele. *Rule Makers, Rule Breakers*. New York: Simon & Schuster, September 11, 2018.

- Gleick, James. *Chaos: Making a New Science*. New York: Penguin Publishing Group, 1988.

- Holland, John. *Complexity: A Very Short Introduction*. Oxford: Oxford University Press, 2014.

- Johnson, Steve. *Emergence: The Connected Lives of Ants, Brains, Cities, and Software*. New York: Scribner, August 28, 2001.

- Kelly, Kevin. *Out of Control: The New Biology of Machines, Social Systems, and the Economic World*. New York: Basic Books, 1992.

- Mitchell, Melanie. *Complexity: A Guided Tour*. Oxford: Oxford University Press, 2009.

- Mok, Kimberley. "Identifying Emergent Behaviors of Complex Systems - In Nature and Computers." *The New Stack*, April 4, 2017. https://thenewstack.io/identifying-emergent-behaviors-complex-systems-nature-computers/.

- Staeger, Steve. "'Desired paths' may be the key to sidewalks at some universities." *9News*, May 24, 2018. https://www.9news.com/article/news/local/next/desired-paths-may-be-the-key-to-sidewalks-at-some-universities/73-557919360.

- Ulanowicz, Robert. *A Third Window: Natural Life beyond Newton and Darwin*. West Conshohocken, PA: Templeton Press, 2009.

- Scott, James C. *Seeing Like A State*. London: Yale University Press, 1998.

CHAPTER 4: HOW EMERGENT ORDER EMERGED

- "Adam Ferguson observed that...." Online Library of Liberty. Accessed February 11, 2021. https://oll.libertyfund.org/quote/adam-ferguson-on-social-structures-not-the-execution-of-any-human-design.

- Axtell, Rob and J. Doyne Farmer. "Predicting the Next Recession." In *Worlds Hidden in Plain Sight: Thirty Years of Complexity Thinking at the Santa Fe Institute*, edited by David C. Krakauer, 243-47. Santa Fe, NM: Santa Fe Institute Press, 2019.

- Buchanan, James. *The Collected Works of James Buchanan Vol. 17: Moral Science and Moral Order*. Indianapolis, IN: Liberty Fund, 2001.

- Chilson, Neil. "A Simplified 'Pretence of Knowledge." *Neil Chilson* (blog). April 4, 2016. https://medium.com/@neilchilson/a-simplified-pretence-of-knowledge-111f5f25a36d.

- Darwin, Charles. *On the Origin of Species by Means of Natural Selection*. John Murray, 1859.

- Discovery Institute. "Charles Darwin: A Short Biography." Accessed February 24, 2021. https://www.discovery.org/a/9511/.

- Hayek, Friedrich. *The Fatal Conceit*. Chicago: University of Chicago Press, 1988.

- Hayek, Friedrich. "The Pretence of Knowledge." Speech presented at the Nobel Memorial Lecture. December, 1974. https://www.nobelprize.org/prizes/economic-sciences/1974/hayek/lecture/.

- Hayek, Friedrich. "The Results of Human Action but not of Human Design." In *Studies in Philosophy, Politics and Economics* by Friedrich Hayek. 96–105. New York: Simon and Schuster, 1967.

- Hayek, Friedrich. "The Use of Knowledge in Society." *American Economic Review*, 35 no. 4 (1945).

- Hayek, Friedrich. "Why I am not a Conservative." In *The Constitution of Liberty: The Definitive Edition*, edited by Ronald Hamowy. Chicago: University of Chicago Press, 1960.

- Henley, William Ernest. *Invictus*. Poetry Foundation. Accessed March 31, 2021. https://www.poetryfoundation.org/poems/51642/invictus.

- Horwitz, Steven. "From Smith to Menger to Hayek: Liberalism in the Spontaneous Order Tradition." *Independent Review*, 6 no. 1, (2001): 81-97.

- *The Iliad of Homer*. Translated by Alexander Pope. Project Gutenberg, 2002. http://www.gutenberg.org/files/6130/6130-h/6130-h.htm.

- Kelly, Kevin. *Out of Control: The New Biology of Machines, Social Systems, and the Economic World*. New York: Basic Books, 1994.

- Maynard Keynes, John. *General Theory of Employment, Interest and Money*. London: Palgrave Macmillan, 1936.

- McChrystal, Stanley. *Team of Teams: New Rules of Engagement for a Complex World*. New York: Penguin Random House, 2015.

- Mises Institute. "Biography of F. A. Hayek (1899 - 1992)." Accessed February 24, 2021. https://mises.org/library/biography-f-hayek-1899-1992.

- Mitchell, Melanie. *Complexity: A Guided Tour*. Oxford: Oxford University Press, 2009.

- Nobel Prize Outreach. "Friedrich August von Hayek." Accessed February 24, 2021. https://www.nobelprize.org/prizes/economic-sciences/1974/hayek/facts/.

- Pool, Robert. "Strange Bedfellows." *Science*, August 1989.

- Roberts, Russ. *How Adam Smith Can Change Your Life*. New York: Portfolio, 2015.

- Santa Fe Institute. "History: Santa Fe Institute." Accessed February 24, 2021.

- Smith, Adam. *An Inquiry Into the Nature and Causes of the Wealth of Nations*. Edited by Edwin Cannan. London: Methuen, 1904. Accessed at Online Liberty Library. https://oll.libertyfund.org/title/smith-an-inquiry-into-the-nature-and-causes-of-the-wealth-of-nations-cannan-ed-vol-1.

- Smith, Adam. *The Theory of Moral Sentiments*. Overland Park: Neeland Media, 2018.

- White, Lawrence H. *The Clash of Economic Ideas*. New York: Cambridge University Press, 2012.

- Yueh, Linda. "Friedrich Hayek's devotion to the free market." *Linda Yueh* (blog). March 23, 2018. https://lindayueh.com/blog/f/friedrich-hayeks-devotion-to-free-markets.

CHAPTER 5: LEADERSHIP WITHOUT CONTROL

- Backman, Elaine and Kate Isaacs. "Nimble Leadership." *Harvard Business Review*, July - August, 2019. https://hbr.org/2019/07/nimble-leadership.

- Koch, Charles. *Continually Transforming Koch Industries Through Virtuous Cycles of Mutual Benefit*. Wichita: Koch Industries, 2020.

- Koch, Charles and Brian Hooks. *Believe in People: Bottom-up Solutions for a Top-Down World*. New York: St. Martin's, 2020.

- Kruse, Kevin. "What is Leadership." *Forbes*, April 9, 2013. https://www.forbes.com/sites/kevinkruse/2013/04/09/what-is-leadership/?sh=3a9aae325b90.

- Manville, Brook. "Why Leadership Can't Be All About You." *Forbes*, July 28, 2019. https://www.forbes.com/sites/brookmanville/2019/07/28/why-leadership-cant-be-all-about-you/?sh=4310d554ae72.

- McChrystal, Stanley. *Leaders: Myth and Reality*. New York: Portfolio, 2018.

- McChrystal, Stanley. *Team of Teams: New Rules of Engagement for a Complex World*. New York: Penguin Random House LLC, 2015.

- Morgan, Jacob. "15 Top CEOs Share Their Definition of 'Leadership,'" What's Yours?" *Medium*, August 13, 2020. https://medium.com/jacob-morgan/14-top-ceos-share-their-definition-of-leadership-whats-yours-2b89a58576a6.

CHAPTER 6: YOUR ROLE IN EMERGENT SYSTEMS
- Building A Second Brain. "Building A Second Brain FAQ." Accessed April 1, 2021. https://www.buildingasecondbrain.com/.

- Coase, Ronald. "The Nature of the Firm." *Economia*, 4 no. 16, (November, 1937): 386-405.

- Sisson, Patrick. "Amazon's bonkers warehouse and delivery empire, by the numbers." *Curbed*, November 26, 2019. https://archive.curbed.com/2017/11/21/16686150/amazon-black-friday-prime-warehouse-delivery.

- Sparks, Daniel. "Amazon's Record 2019 in 7 Metrics." *Motley Fool*. February 6, 2020. https://www.fool.com/investing/2020/02/06/amazons-record-2019-in-7-metrics.aspx.

- "Standards." *xkcd: A Webcomic of Romance, Sarcasm, Math, and Language*. Accessed April 6, 2021. https://xkcd.com/927/.

- U.S. Department of Veterans Affairs. "About VA." Accessed February 24, 2021. https://www.va.gov/about_va/.

- U.S. Department of Veterans Affairs. "Functional Organizational Manual." Accessed February 24, 2021. https://www.va.gov/ofcadmin/docs/VA_Functional_Organization_Manual_Version_2.0a.pdf.

CHAPTER 7: EMERGENT LEADERSHIP IN PUBLIC POLICY

- Chilson, Neil. "Why Joe Biden and Donald Trump are both wrong about Section 230." *Protocol*, November 13, 2020. https://www.protocol.com/biden-trump-section-230-repeal.

- Federal Trade Commission. "Our History: Federal Trade Commission." Accessed February 24, 2021. https://www.ftc.gov/about-ftc/our-history.

- Ha, Anthony. "Brickstream Acquires Nomi for An In-Store Analytics Team Up." *TechCrunch*, October 29, 2014. https://techcrunch.com/2014/10/29/brickstream-acquires-nomi/.

- Hamilton, Alexander. Federalist No. 1. In *Federalist Papers: Primary Documents in American History. Library of Congress*, Accessed April 9, 2021. https://guides.loc.gov/federalist-papers/text-1-10.

- Hayek, Friedrich. "Competition as a Discovery Process," *Quarterly Journal of Economics*, 5 no. 3, (2002).

- Litten, Elizabeth. "When Privacy Policies Should NOT Be Published - Two Lessons From the FTC's Nomi Technologies Case." Fox Rothschild. Accessed April 1, 2021. https://dataprivacy.foxrothschild.com/2015/05/articles/privacy-policies/when-privacy-policies-should-not-be-published-two-easy-lessons-from-the-ftcs-nomi-technologies-case/.

- Manne, Geoffrey. "The Dark Side of the FTC's Latest Privacy Case, In the Matter of Nomi Technologies." *International Center for Law and Economics*. April 29, 2015. https://laweconcenter.org/resource/the-dark-side-of-the-ftcs-latest-privacy-case-in-the-matter-of-nomi-technologies/.

- Ohlhausen, Maureen K. "Remarks to the American Enterprise Institute." Presented at the American Enterprise Institute, Washington D.C., April, 2015. https://www.ftc.gov/system/files/documents/public_statements/635811/150401aeihumilitypractice.pdf.

- Ohlhausen, Maureen. "Dissenting Statement of Commissioner Maureen K. Ohlhausen In the Matter of Nomi Technologies Inc. Matter No. 1323251." Federal Trade Commission, Accessed February 12, 2021. https://www.ftc.gov/system/files/documents/public_statements/799571/150828nomitechmkostatement.pdf.

- *Online Etymology Dictionary.* "govern." Accessed March 1, 2021. https://www.etymonline.com/word/govern.

- Scott, James C. *Seeing Like A State.* London: Yale University Press, 1998.

- Silver, Nate. *The Signal and the Noise: Why So Many Predictions Fail - but Some Don't.* New York: Penguin Group, 2012.

CHAPTER 8: CASE STUDIES

- Facebook. "Facebook Reports Third Quarter 2020 Results." Accessed February 16, 2021. https://investor.fb.com/investor-news/press-release-details/2020/Facebook-Reports-Third-Quarter-2020-Results/default.aspx.

- Facebook. "Facebook's Apps Helped People Celebrate the New Year Together, Even When Apart." Accessed

February 16, 2021. https://about.fb.com/news/2021/01/
new-years-eve-celebration-stats/.

- Oversight Board. "Oversight Board." Accessed March 31,
  2021. https://oversightboard.com/.

- Reddit. "Reddit's 2020 Year in Review." Accessed February
  16, 2021. https://redditblog.com/2020/12/08/reddits-2020-
  year-in-review/.

- Brandeis, Louis and Samuel Warren. "The Right to Privacy." *Harvard Law Review*, 4 no. 193, (1890): 193 - 220.

- Chilson, Neil and Casey Mattox. "[The] Breakup Speech:
  Can Antitrust Fix the Relationship Between Platforms
  and Free Speech Values." *Knight First Amendment Institute*, March 5, 2020.

- Chilson, Neil. "Seeing (Platforms) Like a State." Forthcoming in the Catholic University Journal of Law and
  Technology.

- Chilson, Neil. "When Considering Federal Privacy
  Legislation." *Pepperdine Law Review*, 47 no. 917, (2020):
  917-944.

- Gellerman, Bruce. "'It Was Like A War Zone:' Busing in
  Bost." *WBUR*, September 5, 2014. https://www.wbur.org/
  news/2014/09/05/boston-busing-anniversary.

- Kaplow, Louis. "Rules Versus Standards: An Economic
  Analysis." *Duke Law Journal*, 42, (1992): 557 – 629.

- Klonick, Kate. "The New Governors: The People, Rules, and Processes Governing Online Speech." *Harvard Law Review*, 131, no. 1598, (April, 2018).

- Masnick, Mike. "Protocols, Not Platforms: A Technological Approach to Free Speech." *Knight Institute*, August 21, 2019. https://knightcolumbia.org/content/protocols-not-platforms-a-technological-approach-to-free-speech.

- Paresh, Dave. "Zuckerberg says Facebook's future is going big on private chats," *Reuters*, March 6, 2019. https://www.reuters.com/article/us-facebook-zuckerberg/zuckerberg-says-facebooks-future-is-going-big-on-private-chats-idUSKCN1QN2JR.

- Sunstein, Cass R. "Problems with Rules." *California Law Review* 83 (July, 1995): 953 - 1026.

- Solove, Daniel J. and Woodrow Hartzog, "The FTC and the New Common Law of Privacy." *Columbia Law Review*, 114, no. 3, (January, 2011): 585–86.

- Twain, Mark. *The Tragedy of Pudd'nhed Wilson: And, the comedy, Those Extraordinary Twins.* New York: Penguin 2004.

- Wojcicki, Susan. "YouTube at 15: My personal journey and the road ahead," *YouTube*, Accessed February 16, 2021. https://blog.youtube/news-and-events/youtube-at-15-my-personal-journey.

CHAPTER 9: YOUR ACTIONS STILL MATTER: THEY CAN CHANGE YOU

- Babauta, Leo. *The Power of Less: The Fine Art of Limiting Yourself to the Essential.* New York: Hachette, 2008.

- Clear, James. *Atomic Habits: An Easy & Proven Way to Build Good Habits & Break Bad Ones.* New York City: Avery, 2018.

- Chopra, Deepak. (@DeepakChopra), "All great changes a preceded by chaos." Twitter. July 1, 2018, 8:43 AM. https://twitter.com/DeepakChopra/status/1013402730537340929?s=20.

- Elitch, Dave (@daveelitch). "All Rebound (Slow-Mo)." Instagram Photo. March 30, 2021.

- Elitch, Dave. "Bio." *DaveElitch.com.* Accessed February 23, 2021. https://www.daveelitch.com/bio.

- Elitch, Dave. "Lessons." *DaveElitch.com.* Accessed March 31, 2021. https://www.daveelitch.com/teacher.

- Fuqua, Antonie. dir., *The Equalizer.* 2014; Sony Pictures.

- Godin, Seth. *The Practice: Shipping Creative Work.* New York: Portfolio, 2020.

- Harlin, Renny. dir., *The Long Kiss Goodnight.* 1996; New Line Cinema.

- Hickey, Kasey Fleisher. "This is how the creator of Zen Habits changed his life." wavelength. Accessed February 22, 2021. https://wavelength.asana.com/workstyle-zenhabits/.

- Rohn, Jim. "15 of Jim Rohn's Most Motivational Quotes." *Success.* Accessed February 22, 2021. https://www.success.com/15-of-jim-rohns-most-motivational-quotes/.

- The Tim Ferris Show. "The Tim Ferris Show Transcripts: Dave Elitch (#348)." Accessed March 31, 2021. https://tim.blog/2018/11/28/the-tim-ferriss-show-transcripts-dave-elitch/.

CHAPTER 10: YOUR ACTIONS STILL MATTER: THEY CAN CHANGE THE WORLD

- Carlyle, Thomas. *On Heroes, Hero-Worship, and the Heroic in History.* London: James Fraser, 1841.

- Descartes, Rene. *Rules for the Direction of the Mind.* London: OGB, 2011.

- King, Martin Luther. *Stride Toward Freedom.* New York: Harper & Brothers, 1958.

- Levy, David M. and Sandra J. Peart. "The Secret History of the Dismal Science. Part I. Economics, Religion, and Race in the 19th Century." *Library of Economics and Liberty,* January 22, 2001. https://www.econlib.org/library/Columns/LevyPeartdismal.html.

- McTiernan, John. dir., *Die Hard*. 1988; 20th Century Fox.

- National Portrait Gallery. "Rosa Parks: Tired of Giving In." Accessed March 31, 2021. https://npg.si.edu/blog/tired-giving.

- Pietrusza, David. *Silent Cal's Almanack: The Homespun Wit and Wisdom of Vermont's Calvin Coolidge*. CreateSpace, 2008.

- Roberts, Russ. *How Adam Smith Can Change Your Life*. New York: Portfolio, 2015.

CHAPTER 11: YOU NEED YOUR COMMUNITIES AND YOUR COMMUNITIES NEED YOU

- ALS Association. "The incredible history of the ALS bucket challenge." Accessed April 1, 2021. http://webgw.alsa.org/site/PageServer?pagename=GW_edau_ibc_history#gsc.tab=0.

- Cornuelle, Richard. "De-Nationalizing Community," *Philanthropy*, 1996.

- Give Together Now. "What is #GiveTogetherNow." Accessed February 16, 2021. https://givetogethernow.org/.

- Horwitz, Steve. "10 Tips to Facilitate Collective Action From Elinor and Vincent Ostrom," *Libertarianism.org*, May 21, 2021. https://www.libertarianism.org/columns/10-tips-facilitate-collective-action-from-elinor-vincent-ostrom.

- It's Going Down. "COVID-19 Mutual Aid." Accessed February 16, 2021. https://itsgoingdown.org/c19-mutual-aid/.

- Kaiser Permanente. "Our History." Accessed February 23, 2020. https://about.kaiserpermanente.org/our-story/our-history/building-history-like-building-ships.

- Levin, Yuval. *A Time to Build: From Family and Community to Congress and the Campus, How Recommitting to Our Institutions Can Revive the American Dream.* New York: Basic Books, 2020.

- Putman, Robert. *Bowling Alone: The Collapse and Revival of American Community.* New York: Simon & Schuster, 2001.

- Wittner, Michael. "Learning with friends: The spirit of havurah is alive and well." *Jewish Journal*, January 24, 2019. https://jewishjournal.org/2019/01/24/learning-with-friends-the-spirit-of-havurah-is-alive-and-well/.

CONCLUSION

- Lord, Phil and Chris Miller. dir. *The Lego Movie.* 2014; Warner Bros. Pictures.

- Ravikant, Naval. (@Naval). "To write a great book, you must first become the book." Twitter, May 15, 2018, 2:42PM. https://mailbrew.com/library/naval-ravikant/top-tweets-on-reading?t=6208

Made in United States
North Haven, CT
26 April 2022

18591360R00163